PRAISE FOR *DIPLOMA MATTERS*

"*The San Jose, California, experience in raising academic expectations for all students at the high school level is a model for others to consider. Under Linda Murray's leadership, San Jose Unified School District instituted significant reforms in graduation requirements, which resulted in improved college readiness. This is a story worth reading, including the specific implications for districts nationwide.*"

—**Michael W. Kirst,** Emeritus Professor of
Education and Business Administration, Stanford University;
president, California State Board of Education;
author, *Political Dynamics Of American Education*

"*After spending more than four decades in the field of education, I have read a multitude of books on transforming schools into places that work for all kids. Many of those books have been good or excellent, but none has had the power and punch of* Diploma Matters *by Dr. Linda Murray. Linda, who was an extraordinary superintendent, also proves to be a captivating storyteller. The words flow off her pen and onto paper, telling an impressive story of what it takes to get school reform right. Linda tells it like it is, and her untiring support for educating all of the kids is overwhelming. She captures, in a straightforward way, the nuts and bolts of how to do the work of reform. This is a book for practitioners who have seen it all. I've always felt that Linda Murray was an extraordinary educator. Read the book and you will see why.*"

—**Peter J. Negroni**,
senior vice president, College Board

"*As Mayor of San Jose during Dr. Murray's tenure as Superintendent of San Jose Unified School District, I observed firsthand her commitment to ensuring that underserved, low-income students would be given a chance to go to college. Our shared vision of college readiness for all spurred a strong partnership between the city of San Jose and the school district, and we collaborated throughout the years by providing important supports such as after school homework centers. Our partnership and shared vision continues today as we work together as civic leaders to strengthen the vision of college readiness for the most needy students in our city.*"

—**Susan Hammer**,
former mayor of San Jose;
member of the State Board of Education

"A practical, real-life approach that is easily replicated is just what the doctor ordered for education systems across the United States. Dr. Murray has created a marvelous recipe for success within these pages, and her well-articulated experiences are a gift to everyone in pursuit of improving outcomes for students."

—Mark Walker,
managing director of Global Community Affairs,
Applied Materials, Incorporated.

"This book is a definitive 'how to' for effective, meaningful, and lasting school reform."

—Kathy Burkhard,
former president,
San Jose Teachers' Association

Diploma Matters

A Field Guide for College and Career Readiness

By Linda Murray

Foreword by Kati Haycock

JOSSEY-BASS
A Wiley Imprint
www.josseybass.com

Published by Jossey-Bass
A Wiley Imprint
989 Market Street, San Francisco, CA 94103-1741—www.josseybass.com

Jossey-Bass books and products are available through most bookstores. To contact Jossey-Bass directly call our Customer Care Department within the U.S. at 800-956-7739, outside the U.S. at 317-572-3986, or fax 317-572-4002.

Jossey-Bass also publishes its books in a variety of electronic formats. Some content that appears in print may not be available in electronic books.

Library of Congress Cataloging-in-Publication Data

Murray, Linda, 1944-
   Diploma matters: a field guide for college and career readiness / Linda Murray.
      p. cm.
   Includes index.
   ISBN 978-1-118-00914-7 (pbk.)
   ISBN 978-1-118-07732-0 (ebk.)
   ISBN 978-1-118-07733-7 (ebk.)
   ISBN 978-1-118-07734-4 (ebk.)
   1.   College preparation programs—United States.   2.   Universities and colleges—Entrance requirements.   I. Title.
   LB2351.2.M87 2011
   373—dc22

                                                                    2011014365

Printed in the United States of America
FIRST EDITION
PB Printing   10 9 8 7 6 5 4 3 2 1

CONTENTS

FOREWORD

I f I hadn't seen it with my own eyes, I wouldn't have believed it. Several thousand mostly white teachers of mostly black and brown kids on their feet and cheering as their superintendent called them to action on one of the most audacious district-level policy changes of our time: kids would henceforth take the rigorous academic course sequence heretofore required only of those bound for the elite University of California. Mind you, I said "cheering." Not groaning. Not grumbling. Not rolling their eyes or any of the many things that teachers do when their superintendents get what they describe as "hare-brained" ideas.

Of course, the story didn't begin in that gymnasium. It began over a year earlier when superintendent Linda Murray honestly confronted the growing body of research on the harmful effects of the way we "do" high school in America—allowing students too young to know any better to pick and choose their way through high school, often avoiding the challenging courses that would force them to develop the skills and knowledge they would need in the twenty-first century. Indeed, the sad reality in the San Jose Unified School District—like almost every other school district in America—was that adults in the system often exacerbated this problem by choosing who was "college material" and who wasn't, steering many students—especially minority and poor students—away from the tougher courses.

Not prone to issuing edicts, Linda carefully built support for the idea of teaching all students the so-called A–G curriculum required for admission to California's two public university systems. She started with her school board and with the principals whose job it would be to make this work. But she also engaged the union president very early on. "They don't all have to go to a state university," she argued. "In fact many will enter community colleges or technical training or go right into the workforce. But they will be *prepared*, no matter which route they choose."

The point, in other words, was to give San Jose students real choices.

This book is the story of the process of bringing this idea to fruition in a medium-sized urban school district. It provides a close look at many things that have to be done along the way to make a change as sweeping as this one work for students without killing their teachers. It also provides important insights into what ethical leadership looks like at the district level—how such leaders build a shared sense of moral purpose as well as where they push and where they support.

But though it tells a powerful story, *Diploma Matters* is not simply the tale of change in one California school district. The subtitle says "field guide," and that, indeed, is what this book is designed to do: provide a set of tools to help leaders from other communities who want to move in the same direction.

The timing, of course, couldn't be better. After decades of fighting over how many kids should be educated for college and how many for work, political and education leaders in the United States have acknowledged two new realities that make the old fight moot: (1) that the knowledge and skills necessary for success in today's workplace are pretty much the same as those necessary for success in college and (2) that almost all of our young people will need some postsecondary education to secure work that pays a family-supporting wage. Under the leadership of the nation's governors, state education leaders have even gone so far as to fashion a new set of *common* "college and career-ready" standards that will replace the current uneven patchwork of state-generated standards and form the foundation for common examinations.

Although better standards and assessments will help us get the goals right, they don't provide much of a roadmap for the serious changes in teaching and learning that will be necessary to get students to achieve the new standards. After all, our system hasn't been designed to get all students ready for college and careers. How exactly do we go about identifying and dismantling policies and practices that are no longer suitable? How can we get both educators and the public on board? What pieces of the problem should be tackled first?

That's where this field guide can be enormously useful. Not simply because the San Jose case study is itself so instructive but because, after Linda "retired" from San Jose, she assumed the role of superintendent in residence at The Education Trust–West, the California outpost of a national educational advocacy organization, and built a talented team that worked for several years helping other districts in California to move along this same path.

In *Diploma Matters*, readers not only get a window into what Linda's team learned in that hands-on work but also get access to the tools they built along the way. Tools to help educators and community members see the fractured journeys that many students are taking through high school now and the choke points that block many students from upward movement. Tools to organize focus groups and develop communitywide consensus on more productive paths. And planning tools to help make necessary changes in everything from building new master schedules to assessing whether participating schools have adequate science laboratories and building in the necessary supports for struggling students.

Though some of these tools might seem useful individually, they are designed to work comprehensively. And a comprehensive approach is what the nation's superintendents will need if we're to turn around flat achievement patterns in our high schools and close the long-standing gaps between groups that have hobbled our country for too long.

July 2011

Kati Haycock
President, The Education Trust,
Washington, DC

ACKNOWLEDGMENTS

The inspired leaders of The Education Trust—especially Kati Haycock, president, and Russlynn Ali, former executive director of The Education Trust–West—have been my source of inspiration for many years. Kati's impassioned presentation on the devastating gaps in achievement and opportunity for low-income students and students of color across our country—and right in our own backyard—captured the hearts and minds of my educational team in San Jose. She helped catapult us toward a new vision, in which the opportunity to go to college and enter good careers would no longer be available to the privileged few.

On my retirement from San Jose Unified School District, Russlynn asked me to join The Education Trust team and take the San Jose story on the road. Kati's and Russlynn's passion for closing achievement and opportunity gaps was contagious, and what started as a two-year commitment to build on the San Jose experience has led to six years of building the tools presented in this book and making them available throughout the state.

My deep gratitude goes to my colleagues at The Education Trust and The Education Trust–West, who work tirelessly to close achievement gaps every single day and who show me again and again that this work is important and doable; and to the practice team of The Education Trust–West, who have honed the tools we developed together and made them meaningful to those in the field who are committed to this work. Their insights have made these tools powerful agents of change.

Thanks go as well to the people quoted and highlighted in this book who gave their time to be interviewed, especially to Don Iglesias, whose experiences have helped me tell the story of our success.

Finally, my thanks to those who worked with me to bring this book to fruition: Karl Soehnlein, Kevin Clarke, and Christine Murray. They helped me sort out the most important things to share, present them in ways that tell the story, and bring the written words visually alive. In truth, it is they who have helped me find my voice.

PREFACE

Diploma Matters is written for practitioners who believe fully that the K–12 experience should prepare all students equally well for the full array of opportunities that await them after high school. Whatever they choose, high school graduates should be equipped with the knowledge and skills that will make them successful in both college and careers.

This field guide is intended to help state leaders, district superintendents, principals, and other site and district leaders gain a deep understanding of what it takes to ensure that students from all backgrounds have access to a rigorous course of study that leads to college and career readiness. It can also be a useful resource in the higher education arena as part of teacher preparation and administrator leadership programs. The book builds on lessons learned from my experience as superintendent in San Jose Unified School District, a journey that began to unfold in the mid-1990s and continues today, years beyond when I left the district. In these pages, after describing the reform work done in San Jose, I present implementation tools to guide other practitioners as they embark on a similar journey. The tools include an educational opportunity audit designed to comprehensively understand students' current high school experience and the barriers standing in the way of universal access to rigorous coursework and a blueprint for action based on the findings from the educational opportunity audit. These tools have been used in a wide array of California districts as well as in two high schools in Hawaii. Additionally, a glimpse of what an actual audit and blueprint look like is presented in Chapters Seven and Eight to underscore the power of this approach.

Although the initial context of this reform work was a unique situation in California because the University of California and the California State University systems dictate the minimum high school courses necessary to gain entrance to their schools, this field guide is not intended to be California specific. It will be of great value in any state or local district in which the high school course sequence that leads to college readiness can be agreed on by the district and its higher education community. (As of summer 2010, twenty-one states have now aligned graduation requirements with college entrance requirements.)

Most important, the field guide goes beyond setting forth a policy agenda intended to produce college- and career-ready graduates and gets down to the nuts and bolts of how to accomplish it. I hope your journey to this goal will be furthered by this guide.

THE AUTHOR

Linda Murray, PhD, is currently serving as superintendent in residence for The Education Trust–West (ETW) and is responsible for helping to lead the practice work of the organization in California. The work to date has been centered on high school reform to ensure that all California graduates are college and career ready. In addition, Dr. Murray has served on former state superintendent Jack O'Connell's P–16 commission, which was focused on closing achievement and opportunity gaps in California's public schools, and she has been a member of the California Diploma Project Leadership Team, which has aimed to align college- and career-readiness standards across K–12 and all other higher education sectors.

Prior to joining The ETW, Dr. Murray served as superintendent of schools for San Jose Unified School District from 1993 to 2004. Under her leadership, the district raised its graduation requirements in 1998 to meet the University of California and California State University entrance requisites. Dramatic increases in college and career readiness have been documented over the years, with no negative impact on graduation rates. In addition, achievement and opportunity gaps in San Jose Unified are closing across the K–12 spectrum.

Dr. Murray has been responsible for the creation of the educational opportunity audit and blueprint tools that have been used in nine school districts in California to help move the college- and career-ready agenda to successful implementation. Her experiences in implementing college and career graduation requirements in San Jose and an explanation of the tools are the subject of *Diploma Matters*, her first book.

INTRODUCTION

Throughout my thirty-five-year career in public education, I have applauded, congratulated, grasped hands with, and handed over countless gold-sealed pieces of paper to graduating high school seniors. It never fails to be a giddy, wonderful moment. But after the flashbulbs are finished popping, the hugs have been collected, and the hats are no longer flying through the air, what does that piece of paper really mean?

I mean really.

For some, it means the next step is college. For others, it's not so clear. **I'm writing this field guide for them.**

Like many of my colleagues, I've participated in numerous meetings, task forces, conferences, committees, and working groups discussing and debating what to do about the achievement gap that plagues our nation's schools. There is ample evidence that this gap—some would call it a chasm, maybe even a canyon—exists between low-income students and their more advantaged peers, between students of color and their white and Asian peers, in terms of both achievement and opportunity. Right now, those struggling students are far too often being failed by our school systems. In today's public schools, they are most often placed in "tracks" that don't challenge them, filled with dumbed-down courses in which little is expected of them. This not only leaves them unprepared for college, but it also leaves them unprepared for the reality of today's workplace.

High school should be a gateway to a better life, not a gatekeeper.

Too many students in our schools wind up with too few choices, locked in by what was decided for them by a broken system. Year after

> ### Student Voices
>
> "They showed me how to fill out a McDonald's application in my life skills class. They should have taught me how to fill out a college application. Or at least told me what the requirements were."

year, as we pass students out our doors, we've been handing over a diploma that holds an empty promise.

It's time to stop short-changing low-income students and students of color—the very students who are fast becoming the majority of those we educate in California and many other states. These are our most fragile youth. They most often don't start out with a fair shake and they wind up marginalized further by an educational establishment that has basically given up on them.

To me, the heart of the matter is a moral agenda. There is nothing more urgent in America's public schools than giving students from all backgrounds an education that prepares them for college and careers. And this cannot be accomplished if we don't believe that all students deserve to be prepared *equally.*

For a lot of students, high school is a last chance to become part of the promise of America. When our schools fail them, hope dies, too.

SAN JOSE UNIFIED—A SUCCESS STORY

This book begins with a success story. Not my success. *Our* success. Student success.

It's the story of public high school students in San Jose, California, who graduated eligible for college in far greater numbers than ever before. It is the story of a diverse urban district of thirty-two thousand learners who significantly narrowed a long-standing achievement gap between low-income students and their more advantaged peers, between students of color and white and Asian students. It is the story of a superintendent, her school board, administrators, teachers, and the community coming together to demonstrate that *all* students can succeed when the right steps are taken.

Here's a snapshot of what we achieved:

■ Nearly 50 percent of seniors in San Jose Unified School District's comprehensive high schools graduate with the coursework and grades that qualify them for college. That number is up from about 30 percent in 1998, before our reforms began.

■ Statewide achievement indexes for both Latino and white students have risen, and the overall gap between these students has closed by 37 percent.

- Graduation rates are among the highest in the nation for urban schools, even though our requirements for graduation are well above most other school systems.

WHAT DID WE DO?

In the grandest sense, we changed a failing system through an across-the-board, unwavering commitment to setting the same high expectations for all. In more practical terms, what we did was this: we matched our high school graduation requirements with the entry requirements for our public universities.

In California, to qualify for entry into either of the state university systems—the University of California (UC) and the California State University (CSU)—high school graduates must have completed a minimum number of core courses in seven subject areas. These are known as the A–G requirements (see Table I.1). They include math through algebra II, two years of lab science, two years of world language studies, and more. Most high schools, however, require a far lighter course load of their students. California high school graduation requirements are so very low that only two years of math—nothing more challenging than algebra I—are required. Neither lab science nor world languages are required at all. Confronting this disparity, San Jose Unified in 1998 began expecting high school students to enroll in and pass the A–G sequence in order to graduate.

TABLE I.1: UC and CSU A–G Requirements

A	History and Social Science	Two years (one year world history, one year U.S. history or one-half year U.S. history and one-half year civics)
B	English	Four years
C	Math	Three years, four years recommended (algebra, geometry, algebra II)
D	Science	Two years, three years recommended (biology, chemistry, or physics)
E	World Language	Two years (same language), three years recommended
F	Visual and Performing Arts	One year
G	College Prep Elective	One year

You may have your doubts. You may be thinking, "There's no way this can work" or "Just because it worked for your district doesn't mean it will work in mine." I understand that trepidation first-hand.

My career has been focused largely on the students who struggled in school. Prior to coming to San Jose, I had a long career in Broward County, Florida, much of which was aimed at the students most at risk. I served as a school psychologist; an administrator for compensatory education, dropout prevention, and alternative education programs; head of counseling, social work, and other student services; and as associate superintendent of instruction. None of the work was easy, and solutions were often elusive. Low-income students and students of color were the subgroups most affected by schools that didn't expect much of them. Among high school students, I had seen time and again how many became disenfranchised because they were tracked into low-level classes, because adults believed they couldn't do much, or because the system was set up to create and over time exacerbate achievement gaps. In 1993, when I was hired as superintendent in San Jose, I was ready to make a difference.

There was nothing simple about moving toward a vision of graduating students college and career ready. In our attempt to make high school more rigorous, a plan we called "A–G For All," we encountered doubt, dissent, and outright resistance along the way. But through our efforts, we were able to show that a required college- and career-preparatory curriculum *can* work.

Turning big organizations around is hard work. School superintendents who see themselves as reformers have their work cut out for them. As a leader, you have to have a vision and you must be able to articulate it. You have to develop a strong team to share your vision. You have to be a collaborator and a consensus builder. When colleagues throw up their hands and insist it's all impossible, you have to be able to adapt and reassess. You have to be okay with being unpopular. You have to have a thick skin when certain stakeholders doubt your leadership. On one hand you have to be nimble, and on the other you have be willing to stand firm on principle if you're going to make a difference.

I'm here to tell you it can be done.

How to Use This Book

The San Jose story serves as an illustration of how one district began with the vision of college- and career-ready graduates and then made that vision a reality.

In the chapters that follow, I will go over the steps we took: how we began by engaging all those who had something at stake in our students' education; how we scoured all our available data, especially student transcripts, to arrive at a true understanding of what our students' journeys through high school looked like; how we looked at, questioned, and reconsidered our master schedules, course offerings, safety nets, facilities, budget, and more; how our teaching force transformed as a result of these changes; and how we ultimately created and implemented a comprehensive plan of action based on all we had learned.

Our experience in San Jose was trial and error—a lot of flying the plane while building it—because there were no models in place for us to follow. We tried programs that weren't effective and tossed them away in favor of new solutions. Sometimes those got tossed, too. Think of it this way: we spent a long time doing the research and development so that you won't have to.

What we discovered along the way has been transformed into a toolkit developed by The Education Trust–West (ETW), where I have worked since my retirement from San Jose in 2004. The tools in the kit help you examine the current high school experience (educational opportunity audit) and then develop a detailed action plan for reform (blueprint). At The ETW, we started by building the tools from my experience in San Jose, but they have become more powerful as they have been tested in other districts.

Chapters Five and Six will take you step-by-step through the educational opportunity audit and the blueprint. Please visit our Web site, www.edtrustwest.org. There, you can download working audit and blueprint documents to help you through your own district's reform.

CHAPTER ONE

Dispelling the Myths

Myth\mith\, *n. an unfounded or false notion; a person or thing having only an imaginary or unverifiable existence*

—Merriam Webster Dictionary, 2009

lost track of how many times, as we began to institute our curriculum reforms in San Jose, that I heard the protest, "But not everyone goes to college!"

The implication was clear: why are you pushing a college-preparatory curriculum on students who are not bound for higher education? The answer to this question has everything to do with the changing face of the job market.

MYTH 1: A COLLEGE-PREP CURRICULUM HURTS KIDS WHO AREN'T GOING TO COLLEGE

It's relatively easy to explain why a more rigorous academic curriculum, including four years of English and math up through algebra II, will push more students toward college. What is less apparent, but equally relevant, is that the same curriculum is useful—indeed, *necessary*—for students not planning on enrolling in college. The reason? Today's highly paid, skilled jobs demand a more rigorous base of knowledge than at any time in the past.

Too often in high schools across our nation, students are divided into tracks: college prep and general, which includes a hefty dose of low-level academics mixed with a hodgepodge of vocational-technical programs. The conventional wisdom of the declining manufacturing economy hangs on to this day: "You either work with your hands or work with your brains." But that either-or mentality no longer serves student interests. When done right, vocational education—known across the country today as career technical education (CTE)—can help students access higher level math, communication, and reasoning skills by demonstrating how such skills are applied in the context of the workplace. However, what constitutes "done right"? What are the standards? Why are some students challenged to tackle rigorous content and others told not to worry about it? This is indeed a slippery slope.

The fact is, a student whose high school education has prepared him or her for college will have what it takes to enter a career that offers good pay and opportunity for advancement—even if he or she never goes to college. The American Diploma Project (ADP)—an initiative sponsored by Achieve and The Education Trust, two Washington, DC-based educational policy and advocacy organizations—has clearly demonstrated the need for higher standards in secondary education. ADP found that in terms of English language arts and math proficiency, *employers and colleges want the same thing.*

Better Educated = Better Employed

Most good jobs that pay enough to support a family and point toward a meaningful career require some level of postsecondary education or training.

Studies show that students whose education ends with a high school diploma are frequently less able to compete in the job market. They're getting low-end service industry jobs, and they're getting stuck there for life. College graduates, meanwhile, are earning twice as much and can continue to move up the ladder.

Students may not know this data, but they instinctively desire a chance to succeed. The bottom line is that we need to prepare all high school graduates for some kind of postsecondary education or training so that no matter what path they choose, they have real options for success.

Strong math reasoning skills are necessary, for example, to work in the trade industries. Plumbers need trigonometry and physics; sheet metal and construction workers need geometry; auto technicians need physics. Lower-level courses such as "business math" don't teach conceptual thinking skills the way higher math courses can. Strong English programs that foster writing and communication skills and bring students to a twelfth-grade reading level have become essential for workers who must read and comprehend technical manuals. Today's job market has transformed, but schools are not keeping up in preparing students for it. Employers today know how low standards have fallen. To further underscore how college and career preparation are one and the same—and how we are failing students on both counts—consider this ADP finding: many employers consider a high school diploma "little more than a certificate of attendance." Shouldn't diplomas prepare high school students for more than dead-end jobs? Shouldn't we be alarmed and ashamed that way too many kids exit high schools underprepared for college *and* for work? Figure 1.1 clearly shows that higher wage-earning jobs require education beyond high school.

So, although it is true that not everyone is bound for college, it's also true that all students benefit from the skills that traditional college-prep courses teach. This was one of the driving forces behind our A–G reforms in San

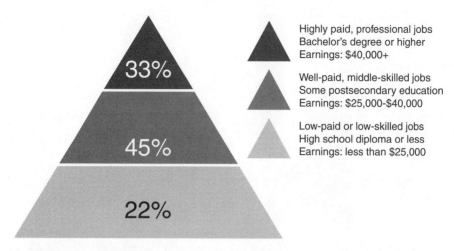

FIGURE 1.1 Defining Workplace Expectations

Source: The America Diploma Project, *Ready or Not, Creating a High School Diploma That Counts.* Washington, DC: Achieve, Inc., 2004. © 2010 The Education Trust–West.

Jose—and why I firmly believe other districts can best serve their students by putting similar standards into place. The time has come to do so.

MYTH 2: THE CURRICULUM WILL BE WATERED DOWN

This myth is based on fear: if all students are enrolled side-by-side in a college-prep curriculum, some believe that students who traditionally have excelled will wind up with a watered-down education.

A lot of this pushback comes from parents whose children are already college bound. They assume that by expecting all students to be challenged to high levels, teachers will end up teaching to the lowest common denominator, which will make school less than challenging, even boring, for their children. Though few parents would dispute the assertion that every student deserves a better opportunity, no one wants to see her own child stagnate while someone else's child catches up.

In San Jose, we carefully monitored our Advanced Placement (AP) and International Baccalaureate (IB) courses to examine and address this fear. It stood to reason that if expectations in the core academic program had been lowered, students would be less prepared to tackle AP and IB in their

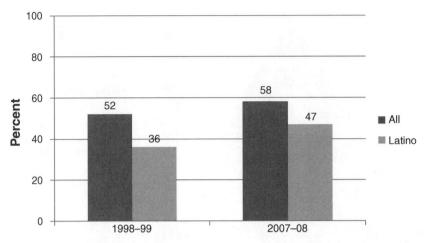

FIGURE 1.2 Percentage of Students Earning at Least Five Credits in AP or IB Has Increased

Source: The Education Trust–West analysis of SJUSD data. *A Case Study: Preparing Students for College and Career,* January 2010. © 2010 The Education Trust–West.

sophomore, junior, and senior years; consequently, there would likely be a drop in enrollments in AP and IB coursework.

In fact, overall AP and IB participation *improved* after instituting A–G For All (see Figure 1.2). Of particular note, Latino students accessed these courses in much higher numbers than previously.

Some have argued that increased participation can be a by-product of changed district policies (such as open enrollment) and that the real measure here would be the pass rates on AP exams. (In other words, if the content of classes leading up to AP were being "dumbed-down" because more students were taking them, then pass rates would have suffered.) However, rather than declining, pass rates on the AP exams in SJUSD have remained nearly the same over the course of a decade even as more students, particularly traditionally underrepresented students, were taking them (see Figure 1.3).

The bottom line: because they were required to take college-prep coursework from day one in high school, more students were ready for college-level classes during their sophomore, junior, and senior years. Further, by providing increased access to the rigorous AP and IB curricula, students were graduating with up to a year of college coursework under their belts. What parents and others feared simply did not come to pass.

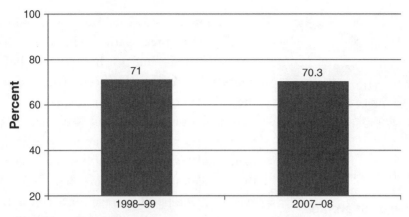

FIGURE 1.3 Percentage of Students Scoring Three or Higher on AP Tests Has Remained Steady

Source: The Education Trust–West analysis of SJUSD data. *A Case Study: Preparing Students for College and Career,* January 2010. © 2010 The Education Trust–West.

MYTH 3: GRADES WILL PLUMMET

I heard a lot about the fears teachers and principals had about instituting A–G For All: "These kids aren't ready for tougher classes. They're going to fail."

Such fears were not unreasonable—higher failure rates would reflect poorly on everyone and would do a disservice to the very students we were focusing on—and arguments ran hot at times. I remember my associate superintendent for instruction saying at one meeting, "Well, if they fail, at least they'll fail something that has meaning to it." But I couldn't deny that by demanding more from our students, we were taking a genuine risk. Still, we held fast to something we heard from students in focus groups that we conducted when we first started thinking about implementing rigorous standards. Again and again, students told us that if more was expected of them, they would work harder. They would rise to the challenge of high expectations.

Think about it from a student's point of view. You're expected to take the same classes as all the other kids in your high school. There you are in this challenging class and the teacher is calling on you to answer the same question she might ask of any of your classmates. You might answer the question right. You might get it wrong. But no one is telling you it's beyond you. No one is telling you that you're not good enough for algebra

0.02%

Change in mean academic GPA for all SJUSD graduating seniors between 1999 and 2008

Despite fears, A–G For All caused no appreciable decrease in grade point average.

and should instead be taking something called "consumer math." The stakes have been elevated—but so has your belief in yourself because you've been given access to the same experience as everyone else.

In San Jose, students *did* work harder and their grades proved it. They did not drop as many had feared. Between 1999 and 2008, as the curriculum became more demanding, the average grade point average for San Jose Unified graduating seniors remained steady.

MYTH 4: STUDENTS WILL DISENGAGE AND DROP OUT

As we began the A–G For All journey, we heard again and again that tough graduation requirements would cause noncollege-bound students to drop out. If we made it too hard on them, they'd disengage and eventually walk away, never to return. That, we were told, was far worse than putting kids in nonchallenging classes. This kind of resistance often took an over-the-top pitch, like a chorus shouting, "The sky is falling!"

Dropouts are an enormous concern for any public school district. When students drop out, they usually don't return. Statistics link dropout rates to unemployment, crime, and teen pregnancy. A kid who drops out is a kid who has given up.

But here's the remarkable news: in San Jose, as coursework became more challenging, graduation rates held steady. As can be seen in Figure 1.4, we didn't lose students because we expected more. Furthermore, San Jose's graduation rates are higher than California's as a whole and have been reported to be among the highest of urban school districts in a national study.[1]

1. Dan Lips, Jennifer Marshall, and Lindsey Burke, *A Parent's Guide to Education Reform* (Washington, DC: The Heritage Foundation, 2008).

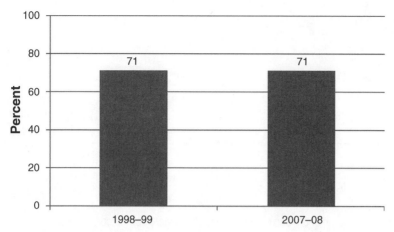

FIGURE 1.4 Graduation Rates Have Not Changed Despite a More Challenging Curriculum

Source: The Education Trust–West analysis of SJUSD data. *A Case Study: Preparing Students for College and Career,* January 2010. © 2010 The Education Trust–West.

MYTH 5: DISADVANTAGED STUDENTS WILL SUFFER THE MOST

Many people believe that students from low-income families, especially students of color, will fail college-preparatory classes in greater proportion than middle- and upper-class white students. This is an example of the entrenched and damaging notion that because some students have not performed well in the past, they can't perform well in the future. In fact, the opposite has proved to be true. Greater rigor—pushing them more than they've been pushed before—actually benefits underrepresented students.

Here is where our data really speaks loudest relative to equity. In a district in which whites traditionally outperformed Latinos, San Jose significantly narrowed the gap between them in terms of the state's Academic Performance Index (API). In addition, as shown in Figure 1.5, Latino graduates have made major gains in AP and IB participation during high school. They are accessing the most rigorous coursework offered in the district in far greater numbers than before the college and career-ready reforms were implemented.

11%

Increase in Latino students earning five or more AP or IB credits

Contrary to concerns, greater rigor actually benefits minority students most.

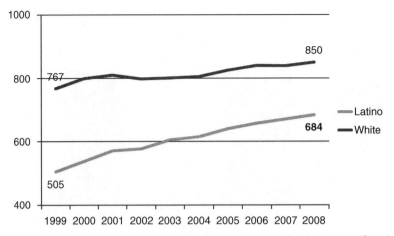

FIGURE 1.5 Latino Students Have Narrowed the Achievement Gap by 37 Percent

Note: With eight hundred being the index that describes proficiency on California standards, there was a steady increase in the API for Latinos and whites and the district's progress in narrowing the achievement gap.

Source: The Education Trust–West analysis of SJUSD data. *A Case Study: Preparing Students for College and Career,* January 2010. © 2010 The Education Trust–West.

MYTH 6: HIGH SCHOOL IS THE WRONG PLACE TO MAKE CHANGES

Even those who understand that a more rigorous curriculum is a worthy goal sometimes protest that high school is the wrong place to start changing expectations. Change has to start in the early and middle grades, they assert, because high school students are too often way behind when they enter. You have to get to them while they're young or you don't stand a chance.

It has often struck me that this myth is employed as a kind of rationalization to do little or nothing at all for students at the high school level. No one doubts that success in the earliest grades will have long-term benefits or that abundant resources must be put into elementary and middle school education to make this happen. But as The Education Trust has observed in their report entitled "Measures That Matter," this kind of thinking has often led to "a serious unwillingness to set very high standards [in high school]" and "inattention to what happens in the basic unit of high school: the

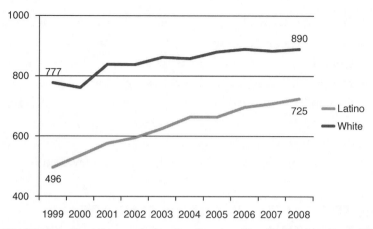

FIGURE 1.6 Test Scores in Earlier Grades Show a Trickle-Back Effect

Source: The Education Trust–West analysis of SJUSD data. *A Case Study: Preparing Students for College and Career,* January 2010. © 2010 The Education Trust–West.

courses students take."[2] In other words, there's an underlying belief that says, if they don't show up prepared, students are beyond help. And that's simply not true.

The truth is that a focus on rigor in high schools sends a clear signal for improving student achievement all the way back to kindergarten, which then makes the pipeline stronger. By shifting expectations, teachers in the early grades work hard to build a solid foundation in basic skills, getting students ready for a college-preparatory high school program.

In San Jose, we found that by demarcating a common set of exit requirements for high school seniors, we created a "trickle-back effect" all the way to the elementary school. And the improvements were remarkable. The gap in API for Latino and white students (looking just at elementary schools) narrowed the most dramatically—by 41 percent (see Figure 1.6). It is noteworthy that Latino elementary achievement on California standards has gone from well below proficiency in 1999 to approaching proficiency by 2008. Overall, elementary schools have shown the largest gains and gap closures compared to middle and high schools in the district.

The biggest reduction in San Jose's achievement gap occurred at the elementary level

Elementary grades benefit from higher standards, too.

2. Achieve and The Education Trust, *Measures That Matter—Making College and Career Readiness the Mission for High School* (Washington, DC: Authors, 2008), 5.

I call this a "trickle-back effect" purposefully to make the strong case that rigorous exit standards set the wheels in motion in San Jose for reforms from kindergarten up. Those who argue you have to start with kindergarten and then meticulously bring all students to grade-level standards every step along the way in order to achieve college and career readiness for all at the end of the line are dead wrong. We, as a country, have traveled down that path for way too many years and have gotten no closer to graduating the majority of our students with high level skills.

MYTH TO REALITY: HIGHER STANDARDS HELP EVERYONE

I call these concerns *myths* because that's what they are: unfounded, false notions that are simply not true. Our experience proved it. The reality is clear: a curriculum that truly prepares all high school students for college and career does work. In the San Jose Unified School District:

- Graduation rates have remained steady.

- Achievement has risen across the K–12 spectrum.

- Achievement gaps between Latinos and whites have significantly narrowed.

Higher standards and expectations did not lead to a watered-down curriculum or to more dropouts but to many more students mastering content with direct benefit for their college and career potential.

> **Student Voices**
>
> "You need a door or a window. Students will find the motivation; they only need the opportunity."

The success achieved in San Jose by adopting these rigorous requirements has since become a model for other districts—in California and beyond—excited by the notion that students can graduate high school with diplomas that have true value in today's world.

QUICK FACTS

Reports by economists and educators consistently point to the need for post-secondary education.

- In the next decade, eight in ten job openings in the United States will require postsecondary education or training.[3]

- During the current downturn, high school graduates are more than twice as likely as college graduates to be unemployed, and that gap has been increasing.[4]

- Forty-five percent of the fastest-growing occupations in the next ten years require a bachelor's degree or higher.[5]

- By 2018, 63 percent of job openings will require workers with at least some postsecondary education or training.[6]

- College graduates earn almost twice the income of high school graduates, and that gap has been increasing.[7]

- For every additional average year of schooling per student, the U.S. gross domestic product (GDP) would increase by about 0.37 percentage points—or by 10 percent—over time.[8]

● READER REFLECTION

1. Did the data about dispelling myths in San Jose Unified surprise you in any way? How?

2. Which data presented the most compelling evidence that a college- and career-ready curriculum should be a goal for all students?

3. What are the implications of San Jose's experience for other districts seeking to pursue an equity agenda around equal access to better education and opportunity?

3. Arne Duncan, "Reform, Accountability, and Leading from the Local Level" (speech presented at the National League of Cities' Congressional City Conference, Washington, DC, March 15, 2010).
4. Hans Johnson, *Educating California: Choices for the Future* (San Francisco: Public Policy Institute of California, 2009).
5. U.S. Department of Labor, Bureau of Labor Statistics (BLS), *Occupational Outlook Handbook* (2010–11) (Washington, DC: Government Printing Office, 2010); U.S. Department of Labor, Bureau of Labor Statistics Employment Projections 2008–2018 (Washington, DC: Government Printing Office, 2009).
6. A. P. Carnevale, N. Smith, and J. Strohl, *Help Wanted: Projections of Jobs and Education Requirements Through 2018* (Washington, DC: Georgetown University, Center on Education and Workplace, 2010).
7. Ibid.
8. D. T. Jamison, E. A. Hanushek, and L. Woessmann, "Education and Economic Growth," *Education Next*, 8, no. 2 (2008): 62–70.

CHAPTER TWO

Expectations Matter

"Girls don't do well in higher math."

Back in 1961, when I was a high school junior in Rochester, New York, I told my teacher, Mr. Moynihan, that I wouldn't be enrolling in precalculus during my senior year because I thought that girls didn't do well in higher math.

I was a good student in high school. My grades were in the B+ range, and my grades in math were especially strong. So why was I opting out? Well, at Greece Olympia High School, not a single female student—not one—was enrolled in precalculus, the capstone math course during those years. I'd clearly absorbed this fact, and I'd accepted the message underlying it: higher math was beyond me, as it was beyond any girl in my class.

Fortunately for me, Mr. Moynihan didn't accept my explanation. He saw plainly what I couldn't: I had the capacity to succeed. And that's how, in my senior year, pushed by an astute teacher, I was the first female in my high school enrolled in precalculus.

I remember the feeling of exhilaration at being given a chance I hadn't expected—mixed in with the fear that I would prove the conventional wisdom right. I was afraid that my failure would represent a failure for anyone who tried to move beyond expectations (to say nothing of the way that I might disappoint my teacher). I remember, too, the isolation of being singled out in this way, an inadvertent trailblazer. As it turned out, I struggled with precalculus, but not any more than I struggled with any new concept. In the end, was higher math beyond my capability? Absolutely not.

Almost fifty years later, we have to a large extent moved beyond segregating students into academic coursework based on gender. Yet tracking low-income students and students of color into lower-level classes still happens way too often in America's schools. Built-in assumptions still create self-fulfilling prophecies. Teachers and administrators pass on their low expectations to certain students who internalize them, making success nearly impossible. How can students rise to the challenge if they are not exposed to challenging material?

SETTING THE FOUNDATION FOR REFORM

There's no way to fully explain how we challenged these ingrained expectations in San Jose without delving into a little bit of history. In the 1960s, similar to so many other urban areas across the United States, San Jose suffered from the phenomenon of "white flight." SJUSD became a district whose schools were largely segregated: white, affluent students lived in the suburban Almaden Valley and poor and working class Latino students lived closer to the center of the city. This residential segregation between "Valley" and "downtown" students showed up as a gap in grades, performance, and graduation rates, as well. Between the late 1960s through the late 1980s, various studies, lawsuits, and court orders attempted to address this inequity.

When I arrived in 1993, the district was in its eighth year of court-ordered desegregation. Components of this included a busing scheme based on choice, with families choosing the school where they sent their kids—transportation provided by the district. The plan called for the creation of magnet-like themed schools—for example, schools devoted to science, the visual and performing arts, a Montessori structure, and two-way language immersion.

The district had begun to confront the achievement gap that existed between its most affluent students and its most disenfranchised. In 1992 SJUSD partnered with the College Board in Equity 2000, an initiative spread out over six sites across the country that was dedicated to the idea that all students could successfully complete algebra and geometry—the two major gatekeeper courses to college access.

As a result, when my tenure began in 1993, San Jose Unified had eliminated all math courses below algebra from its ninth-grade offerings. Gone were "consumer math" and other dumbed-down math classes. Not only were all beginning high school students required to take algebra but also—to the surprise of many—the nontraditional algebra takers were passing it at the same rate as they had passed consumer math! This early success demonstrated that all students could enroll and be successful in algebra, a course that had been considered by many to be beyond the grasp of students who struggled in math. It was nothing short of eye-opening.

At the same time, those kids who couldn't immediately rise to the challenge were given extra support—"safety net" programs, such as Saturday academies, tutorials, shadow classes (which gave struggling students a daily support class in a subject with which they had difficulty), and after-school and summer extension classes—so that we weren't bypassing anyone in order to meet our overall goals. The powerful lessons learned in those early days would become essential when it came time to implement a comprehensive, college-ready curriculum for all students.

This was a strong foundation. But there was still much work to be done.

FINDING COMMON GROUND

When I arrived in San Jose, I learned what it really means to be on the front lines of reform. The school district introduced me to the community at a very crowded open board meeting. I was welcomed by the board with flowers; the press took pictures. Then it was time for the community to speak at the open microphone, and I quickly understood why the room was packed.

In attendance was a large contingent from the Latino community, every one of them angry at my appointment, many of them lined up to speak their minds. And speak they did. How could this have happened? they wanted to know. You can't represent our needs and interests, I was told. My appointment was seen as evidence of a nonresponsive board's continuing lack of attention to the needs of Latino students, another slap in the face to an already disenfranchised community. The message to me was clear: *regrese a casa*. Resign and go home. We don't want you here.

When the public commentary ended, I stood up and walked across the room, wading into the opposition. I held out my hand, and I said something like, "I want to know where this anger comes from, this distrust. I want to listen to you. I will get in a room with whomever you want to bring. I promise we will meet as often as you want—if you do one thing for me. Bring me a list of the ten things that are most important to you. If you're willing to do that, we have a place to start."

And they did. They brought a list to our first meeting. The first item was something I addressed immediately: adding a Spanish-speaking Latino administrator to my cabinet, someone whom the community saw as representative of their experience. I made her an associate superintendent. The second item was the establishment of a Latino advisory committee with which I would meet regularly. I brought staff with me to every one of these meetings so that it wasn't just an empty exercise, and these staffers always left with a list of action items.

These changes rapidly transformed my relationship with the people who once saw me as their adversary. Listening to them, I learned why they felt excluded, pushed out, not valued. They felt they'd been knocking on the district's door with no answer for years. They had big, difficult, complicated concerns—such as the way Latino students were systematically relegated to low-level tracks and excluded from college-prep classes. Or the way bilingual and special education programs were not serving their needs.

The point of all this is not that I did anything particularly heroic or that there was ultimately anything suspect about the group that opposed me at that first board meeting. The point is, we both brought something of value to the table, and we learned to listen to each other. By the end of my first year, I knew that community pretty well, and I had begun to earn their trust. Everything grew from that.

In early 1994, another opportunity arose for us to take a step forward. A new judge had given us the go-ahead to write out a "consent decree"—a legal agreement between the district and the plaintiffs in the desegregation lawsuits—which essentially would spell out the steps the district would take during the next few years to end court oversight. This presented the opportunity to shift the focus away from assigning students to schools for the purpose of ethnic integration and instead move toward closing the achievement gap. The decree required an aggressive effort to increase minority participation in honors, AP, and IB classes. Parental involvement was also a required component; we wanted to ensure that parents of Latino students would begin to see the possibility of college in their children's futures and push for high achievement now.

We took ten months to hammer out the consent decree. I had a heavy hand in its writing. Most superintendents wouldn't get anywhere near that table full of lawyers arguing point by point, but I believed, as did the plaintiffs in the desegregation lawsuit, that insidious practices such as tracking had to be eliminated. This struck me as a clear way to gain a major weapon in our reform arsenal—the authority of the courts—which would *mandate* the changes that I saw as essential to moving the district forward toward college and career readiness for all. I'll admit that I was unabashedly opportunistic here. Opportunism is, as I see it, an essential component of being a reformer and it's a theme I'll return to again in this book.

The foundation for San Jose's later success was laid in these early years. I would not have succeeded if my agenda had been to force sweeping changes from the top down. Or could reform have happened solely as a grassroots mobilization without committed, established leadership looking for every chance to move the agenda forward.

None of us could achieve anything to better the lives of the district's students unless the effort came from both directions—unless we stepped together onto common ground.

A DEFINING MOMENT: THE STUDENTS SPEAK

Expectations matter. In San Jose, we heard again and again stories from students that confirmed this basic truth. As my school board and I zeroed in on the University of California's A–G requirements, they became the rallying cry for our vision. The requirements are clear and easy to articulate (see Chapter One) and they essentially set the bar for what students are expected to know when they graduate if they pursue college as their goal—or as the research suggests, if they are to enter today's workplace with a real chance for advancement beyond entry-level jobs. Although the A–G requirements have harsh critics—who, among other concerns, maintain that universities shouldn't dictate what high school students should have to take to graduate—we felt that in terms of setting our policy, this was the right place to put our stake in the sand.

One evening, members of the board and I stood together behind a two-way mirror and watched a facilitator talk to a group of high school students about their experiences in our district's high schools. It was the single most powerful factor in our decision to make college-ready curricula available to all.

The students were there as part of a series of focus groups we conducted to take the temperature for the changes we were contemplating. The make-up of this student group was diverse, representational of the thirty-two thousand students in our district. Some were from the suburban area of the district, the children of wealthy engineers and corporate executives; some were the children of immigrant families in downtown San Jose, who struggled to make ends meet.

Through that two-way mirror, this is what we heard:

- "Teachers don't care."
- "School is boring."
- "It is easy to get through high school without doing much."
- "Nobody pushes you to excel—it's all up to you."
- "I could do a lot more if I was asked to."

Talk about low expectations!

No matter what their background, they had no disagreement when they spoke: they didn't think they were getting a good education. They could do more if more was asked of them. It was too easy to slide by if you chose.

I remember one student in particular, who clearly marched to his own drummer—he'd shown up wearing a cape, making a statement about his individuality. As soon as I saw him, I thought, this one is going to be a wiseguy. But he turned out to be very articulate in depicting how mediocrity is rewarded. This was a young man who attended one of our more affluent schools, whose parents, I assumed, would be pushing him to the nth degree. But his claim was that aside from self-motivation, he felt no push from anyone else to excel. That surprised me. It made me realize that what we were confronting was more than an opportunity gap between ethnic and socioeconomic groups. Our challenge was to take *all* kids, regardless of their background, and push them toward their full potential.

Years later, after we implemented the college-and career-ready curriculum for all, the students I interviewed about their high school experience were telling a different story. One high school senior said, "I really appreciate how the administration in our school is pushing kids . . . . They are expecting a lot, and I think it's a good thing." Another senior explained that she had been motivated "since freshman year . . . to aim higher than I had expected for myself."

When I think about why other districts should take on what we did in San Jose, I remember the words of these students. The difference between what they said before and after we ratcheted up our graduation requirements is the clearest illustration of our success. Before, we had too many students spiraling in a sinkhole of underachievement. After, we had a much greater number of students excelling. Before, they were internalizing low expectations. After, they were buoyed up by systemwide support that sent the message loud and clear: you are capable of more than you've ever believed.

Listening to that student focus group catapulted me to the next level. I had always believed public schools could do more, particularly for underserved students. After that view through the two-way mirror, I felt it viscerally, and I knew we had to raise the bar and level the playing field.

HOW GOOD IS GOOD ENOUGH?

How did we get there? Slowly. We knew right away that we needed to work more closely with community stakeholders to educate them and gain their support for such a move. With the assistance of Public Agenda, experts on public opinion research, we were able to put together a comprehensive public engagement strategy to test the waters and ask this question of all district stakeholders: "In San Jose Unified School District, how good is good enough?"

We brought together not only teachers and students but also parents—from the suburbs, from urban neighborhoods, from families in which only Spanish was spoken—as well as district residents who had no students in high school. After seven sessions that probed whether the district was delivering a "good enough" education, we heard a very loud, very clear response: "No." Every group was in agreement. It was time to raise our standards—a *common* set of standards for all high school students that would ensure them a meaningful diploma.

Although teachers supported higher expectations for high school students, they were the most skeptical. They worried about their ability to implement a college-preparatory curriculum for all students. They feared they would fail at their jobs if they were given kids whom they'd traditionally never seen succeed. The teachers made clear that they could implement this curriculum only if sufficient support was in place, meaning quality professional development along with strong student support systems. Addressing these concerns became a critical component of our reform efforts.

Focus group research set us up for our next major public engagement initiative, a town hall meeting that we called a "community conversation." With the help of Public Agenda and the Institute for Educational Leadership, we brought together a group of 150 broadly representative parents, teachers, and community leaders to explore our questions in depth.

Though we held our meeting at a downtown location on what turned out to be a rainy Saturday morning, attendees came from far and wide. Across the board, participants expressed their wishes that *all* students in San Jose Unified receive an excellent education. They clearly saw that the district should prepare every student to have the choice of college in their future. We walked away from that conversation convinced that our major stakeholders were ready for San Jose Unified to move down this path. After the community conversation, we sent a follow-up written survey to all high school parents, students, and teachers that echoed what we'd heard in person. We knew we had a mandate to proceed.

Some would call this public engagement work *consensus building;* I prefer the phrase *common ground.* Whatever the terminology, it is clear that finding out what the public is thinking on matters of great importance is critical to reform work. To truly lead, you have to trust the public to engage in thoughtful, civil debate on issues for which there are no easy answers.

GETTING THE TEACHERS' UNION ON BOARD

This book would not be complete without acknowledging backroom politics. Although the focus groups and community conversations were bringing our mandate into sharper clarity, we were also working behind the scenes with the teachers' union. I'll have more to say in Chapter Four about the role of teachers in implementing college- and career-ready requirements, but for now it's worth mentioning some critical early steps.

When I began my tenure as superintendent, a long-standing contentious relationship existed between the district office and the San Jose Teachers' Association. I saw that reform was possible but only if trust could be rebuilt, and that meant devoting plenty of time and energy to mending this fractured relationship. Both the president of the union and I had to be willing to put aside power and control in our personal relationship with one another. We knew this would force us to step outside our traditional roles, so that we could better understand each other's fundamental responsibilities as leaders of demanding constituencies. We needed to be able to "walk in each other's shoes" and work with each other's interests in mind. This

---

Student Voices

"I was planning to make my life really easy in high school and just enjoy it and learn English. I didn't know I had to take all the English, math, and science. As I look back, I think: what was I thinking? The A–G requirements help you, they build you, and they make you who you are until now."
—Latina graduate, 2004

"You need a door or a window. The A–G curriculum gives you that opportunity. I can't imagine not having it. Students will find the motivation . . . they only need the opportunity."
—Latino graduate, 2004

"Everyone should have the A–G courses. You may not go to college, but you have the option. I think it's wonderful."
—Middle Eastern student from San Jose High Academy, 2008

was a tall order, especially when lofty goals for students began to buck up against the rights of teachers, which had been collectively bargained.

But we had a unity of purpose—to close achievement gaps and prepare students for college and career—so we met behind closed doors on a regular basis to problem solve, finding win-win solutions on many of the thorny issues that had historically created tension between the district and union members. Over time we came to understand that we *could* work together on behalf of both students and teachers.

Dramatic change and real reform cannot happen in isolation of teachers' unions, which exert great influence over their members. In San Jose, union leaders generated teacher buy-in for the A–G graduation requirements. They determined how to message the new expectations, which allowed them to get their members on board without fanfare or drama. The leadership assured their members that the district planning process was thoughtful, thorough, and had teachers' needs at the forefront. At our weekly meetings, the president and I grappled with their most pressing concerns, such as what to do about English learners and special needs students. We agreed to bring teachers in on every step of the planning process, and we did just that. We allowed them as much autonomy as possible at the site level, giving departments flexibility about how to implement the new course requirements. We listened carefully to their requests for student safety nets and for site-based professional development and we actively planned together on how to deliver on their requests (see Chapter Four). We went out together on weekly visits to high schools and talked to teachers about why this was so important and sought out their concerns so that we could continue to address them.

As a result, teachers, by and large, did not perceive the reform to be simply a top-down mandate so they did not push back. This allowed us to move forward without insurmountable serious issues, though of course there were challenges along the way. Although we managed to navigate our way through the buy-in process with most teachers, I cannot emphasize enough that teacher buy-in (and counselor buy-in, too) is the thorniest issue in any high school reform. The union president and I knew some of the old guard would never come along, so we came up with an agreement to offer them a retirement incentive. The incentive included an annuity over five years and benefits until age sixty-five. It more than paid for itself because the cost of replacement teachers was so much cheaper than veterans. And the teachers who most opposed the changes went out with dignity and a reward for loyal service. Of course, we lost a few great ones in the process, but the energetic, reform-minded teachers who entered the district provided an infusion of new blood.

In my post–San Jose work, the most resistance that I have encountered has come from math teachers, but interestingly, this was not the case in San Jose. As discussed previously, the district had already implemented algebra for all in the early 1990s. There had been a lot of resistance from math teachers in those days, but after five years, with change established, including safety nets and professional development, math teachers became strong supporters. They had experienced success with algebra and were ready to push beyond into higher-level math. They made a positive impact on their colleagues in other disciplines, who became more open to changing their own beliefs.

There's no magic potion to transforming the hearts and minds of nonbelievers. There are, however, multiple channels of communication and strategic moves to be explored and developed together, which can in the end lead to remarkable changes.

From Combat to Collaboration

Some Thoughts from Kathy Burkhard, Former Teachers' Union President

When Dr. Murray arrived in SJUSD in 1993, there was a long history of combat and distrust between the district and the teachers' union. We were negotiating a new contract; bargaining was stalled and we were preparing to strike.

The most contentious issue was teachers' salaries. Teachers had always been an afterthought in the budgeting process rather than a priority. Dr. Murray changed that when she came to the table with a "FairShare Formula." The formula secured our place as a legitimate budget expenditure and acknowledged our right to a percentage of district revenues. She opened up the district's books and welcomed analysis. The strike was averted and we began to move toward a culture of problem solving and trust.

When the conversation began about the A–G requirements, it was a no-brainer. Why wouldn't teachers want rigorous standards? However, we did have legitimate concerns, specifically that the burden would fall onto teachers without any additional help. But promises for safety nets and other support systems materialized. In the days before "the enlightenment," teachers never would have believed the district's promises. Pushback and rancor would have been inevitable.

But because of the trust that had been established, we could assure our members that there would be help, not blame. It took the union trusting the district to make the transition to A–G a smooth one. In the end, the new standards were a win for everyone.

SETTING OUR STAKE IN THE SAND

You have to do it somewhere. Say, "That mark there, that's our goal. We *will* have different expectations for the class of 2012 than we had for the class of 2011." It doesn't matter how far away you plant that stake in the sand—two years down the road, five years down the road. What matters is that at some point, the outcome has to be non-negotiable. The stake says, "We're never going back."

Our stake in the sand was the non-negotiable outcome that students would be expected to take and pass the college- and career-ready courses to graduate. In January 1998—after three years of meetings, studies, focus groups; three years of struggling our way through politics, resistance, and fear in order to find common ground—the San Jose Board of Education adopted the UC system's entrance requirements (A–G) as our graduation requirements, to begin with the entering freshman class of 1998.

It was time for the real work to begin.

⬤ READER REFLECTION

1. How important are teachers' unions in successful school reform?

2. How important are adult expectations in determining how much students achieve? Explain.

3. Should all students take a core curriculum that prepares them to go to college if they choose, or should requirements allow some students to take a less rigorous high school course load?

CHAPTER THREE

The Journey Through High School

HOW DO YOU TURN IDEAS INTO ACTION?

It's one thing to decide that you want to close the achievement and opportunity gaps in your district. It's another thing to make it happen. I'm embarrassed to admit that at the very beginning of our efforts, part of me imagined that what we had to do would be simple. After all, we shared a proud vision of improving the education of all students in our district. But like many things of value, the grander the vision, the more complicated the implementation.

Moving from idea to action is a process, and that process starts with a clear understanding of where you're starting from. In our case, we needed an accurate picture of our students' journeys through high school. Before we could change the way we educated our students, we had to educate ourselves *about* our students.

Why do achievement and opportunity gaps exist? You might have your own theories; you might even have anecdotal evidence. But the deepest understanding of the problem is going to come from looking closely and methodically at the reality of your district as it exists today. Every district has its own unique profile, its own set of needs. In San Jose, we developed a process that helped us—and by extension can help you.

We knew we had to use all available data. We set up a central location—we called it the "war room"—where our team met to share and compare that data. And we started asking questions like these:

- What do students know when they show up for freshman year?
- How does that first year set the patterns for the years that follow?
- Is there notable, disproportional under-representation in college-preparatory curricula for students of color, low-income students, and English learners?
- Where are the most serious choke points—those courses in which students experience failure as they move through high school—and what happens to students when they encounter one?
- Are there interventions in place to catch kids before they fall through the cracks?

- How do students get placed in college-preparatory courses?
- What do typical course-taking patterns reveal about successes and failures?
- What does senior year look like?

Cumulatively, we were trying to identify what the journey through high school was like for students in our district.

THE WAR ROOM

In San Jose, our war room wasn't as high-tech as what army generals are used to—in fact, it wasn't high-tech at all. This was the mid-1990s and our technology was to some degree still crude. But the metaphor seemed apt because everyone involved knew this was a fight we couldn't afford to lose.

The conference room where we met became our command central: a place to institute a long-term strategic view and a shorter-term tactical plan to nail down how to get from here to there. *This* was the place where we were going to turn our ideas into action. We had charts plastered all over the room filled with facts and data. The team met every couple of weeks and when we hit a wall, we'd part with our next assignments. No one left the war room without a task, which usually involved gathering up more data to help us fill the holes in our charts.

In the end, it seemed less like a war room and more like a haven for creative brainstorming: a place to gather and analyze data, to understand what the data were showing us, and to think creatively about solutions.

ANALYSIS OF STUDENT TRANSCRIPTS

The first and most important thing we did was look at student transcripts. We learned so much. Transcripts contain a wealth of information far too rarely mined in any systematic manner. We tend to think of transcripts as individual reports, but if you look at enough of them together, larger patterns emerge—for example, patterns in course-taking for students who pursue college versus students who don't. Set a group of transcripts from poorly performing students side-by-side, and you'll quickly identify the choke points in your curriculum—those courses that turn out to be obstacles on the journey through high school for many students. You'll also learn pretty quickly whether anything is in place to intervene in a timely manner to reverse patterns of failure and poor achievement. Transcripts can reveal exactly how a lack of access to college and career-preparatory coursework manifests itself among poor students, students of color, special needs students, and English learners. In short, transcripts tell us whether our schools are organized in ways that promote high student expectations or in ways that leave the majority of students accomplishing only the minimum.

Student transcript analyses in San Jose provided us with a startling picture of what happened to students as they moved from the beginning of high school to graduation. We culled a representative sample of transcripts from the most recent graduating class and discovered some sobering truths:

- The majority of our students took the least-challenging academic course load and minimum number of credits to get by—which directly related to why they were graduating neither college nor career ready.

- If students started in a college-preparatory track and struggled, they dropped down to a general track and remained there.

- If they started in a general track and did well, they rarely were pushed up into a college track.

- There was a persistent pattern of lower performance by our largest subgroup, Latino students, and a vast under-representation of Latinos in courses that would prepare them for college and good careers.

- The biggest choke points for noncollege-bound students were in math, and many students had *repeated* failures in the same course (usually algebra).

- Intervention classes were few and far between, and the only intervention clearly apparent in the transcript review was making students repeat a course they had already failed.

- D and F grades were earned at about the same rate for students in both the general track and college track, particularly in English and math.

- No evidence could be found that timely interventions were in place to prevent failure in the first place.

- Few students were involved in career-technical pathways; in most cases, those who ventured into technical fields were doing little more than dabbling in a course or two.

- Senior year for many students was a wasted year, with the majority taking less than a full schedule—even those who were college bound.

Not all of these facts were a complete surprise. We knew there were problems in the district, and for years we had been attempting piecemeal solutions. But only after we got this full picture, based on districtwide transcript analysis, were we able to understand that the foundation of the problem was in our underlying infrastructure. In other words, failing students weren't the problem; the system in which they failed was. This allowed us to understand that any solution we attempted would have to be systemwide. Every identifiable problem in the district was a piece of the whole.

See Chapter Five to learn how you can undertake the process of transcript analysis and discover what transcripts can show you about your district.

THE MASTER SCHEDULE

A high school's master schedule is like the frame of a house—it supports the entire academic structure. Like a house with many rooms, the master schedule can be seen from many different angles, and it's the cumulative picture that reveals what is important to the school.

As we examined our students' journeys, we saw that the way we organized our high schools actually *created* barriers to student success. Incoming freshman, for example, often found themselves placed in large classes. For many, this is their most vulnerable year, when they need the most attention and help. If they began to struggle in these large classes, they were much more likely to slip through the cracks. In comparison, the most advanced upper division classes, such as AP, were significantly smaller in size. This struck us as the inverse of what was needed.

A good master schedule puts students' needs first. I think it's true that a significant number of master schedules don't operate this way. Too often they are built around what teachers want to teach rather than what students need to take—an outgrowth of the way schools are often structured for the benefit of adults rather than kids. Our reforms were strongly driven by a sense that what students need to succeed are higher expectations and standards, and so, in order for our high schools to support students in this new, more rigorous environment, each master schedule had to be studied from the foundation up in order to meet those needs.

In our war room, the master schedules of San Jose's six high schools came under intense scrutiny. Everything was up for discussion:

- Bell schedules
- Teachers' class loads
- Which classes were offered each period
- Availability of college-preparatory classes
- The number of classes offered beyond the minimum for college readiness, including AP and other upper-level courses
- Electives offered
- Singleton classes—those courses that enroll only enough students to make up one section and thus wind up creating problems in access
- Use of block scheduling and other modifications to a traditional six-period day

We looked at all of this with a particular concern for students who struggled in their courses. Now that we had a picture of what the journey through high school looked like, we wanted to see if our master schedules were designed with an eye toward intervention. Was a traditional schedule in the freshmen year conducive to early success? Were support classes built into the day to ensure that students falling behind had opportunities to review the material covered in the main class? Were extra classes available before and after school to provide extra support? What kinds of tutorials were available to students and when? Looked at from another angle, was there any common planning time set aside for teachers in core areas to encourage collaboration?

Our analysis quickly revealed cracks in the foundation:

- Students who most needed the best instructional environment were often in the largest classes with the most inexperienced teachers.

- Because few support classes had been contemplated when the high school master schedule was built, struggling students could not access help during the instructional day.

- Classes were not available outside the usual six-period day to help struggling students.

- Singleton classes often created scheduling conflicts that served as barriers to access to more rigorous courses.

- Most schedules did not provide common planning time within disciplines so teacher collaboration around student needs was minimal.

Both the master schedule and the student transcript analysis sharpened the picture of what the high school journey was like for the majority of our young people—and it wasn't a pretty picture:

- Nearly 30 percent of San Jose's students were sailing through their four years of high school on a college track; those students were mostly white or Asian.

- The rest of the students were sliding by taking the easiest path to the diploma.

- Some of these were hanging on by a thread—if they even made it to their senior year.

These last two groups—a majority of our district's students—were looking at receiving a diploma that lacked meaning, locking them out of pursuing a college degree and good careers in the new economy.

We knew that we needed to put some measures into immediate effect, such as creating smaller classes for students in need of personalized attention and assigning our best teachers to the students who were struggling most. But more significantly, we understood that the changes needed in San Jose would not be small fixes but a structural overhaul.

See Chapter Five to learn how you can undertake the process of looking at your master schedule with an eye toward rebuilding it based on student needs.

JUST-IN-TIME INTERVENTIONS

Looking at the transcripts and master schedules revealed something very important to us: our support and safety nets were lacking in any *systematic* impact. Nothing was in place to trigger an intervention with a particular student who was struggling to learn difficult content.

If a student failed a course such as algebra, the most common intervention was that he or she simply repeated it—a second dose, or a third, of the same medicine, often spooned out by the same teacher. If a teacher, counselor, or administrator didn't make a personal effort on behalf of a student, directing him or her toward support as the need became apparent, the reality was that the student might simply fall through the cracks.

Many districts are probably like San Jose was in terms of academic intervention. We had some tutoring support in our high schools. We had in place a smattering of programs designed to support under-represented students in rigorous coursework. (Among these were Advancement Via Individual Determination [AVID], Math, Engineering, Science Achievement [MESA], and Gaining Early Awareness and Readiness for Undergraduate Programs [GEAR UP].) We had established a few partnerships with local nonprofits, businesses, and the City of San Jose that provided after-school support. None of this, however, was enough.

In the new world of college and career preparation for all, we needed something more comprehensive, accessible by all students and, most important, available as soon as a student began to struggle. In San Jose, we tried everything we could think of:

- Saturday academies for students receiving poor grades early in the quarter—an attempt to intervene before a student received an F for a course grade

- Shadow classes that added extra daily support classes for students struggling in math courses and in English language arts

- Extending classes on certain days in order to bank the time for another day, when those hours could be cashed in. Banked minutes were used to help struggling students or give teachers extra time for professional development and collaborative planning.

- Pushing beyond the traditional six-period day. Zero periods in the morning and seventh periods after the last bell were added for kids who needed them. To mitigate the cost, teacher schedules were overlapped, so some teachers came in early and some stayed later.
- Building tutorial periods into master schedules
- Establishing after-school homework centers at every school
- Partnerships, such as an e-mentoring program with IBM employees, for individual students who needed help in math
- Mentoring programs with community volunteers providing ongoing support to cohorts of at-risk students, following them from ninth grade to twelfth grade

Some of these programs, such as shadow classes and homework centers, were implemented at all of our high schools. Others were particular to a specific school. We believed that each site should build comprehensive safety net programs based on the talents and resources that were unique to them and where the school believed it would get the greatest results.

What the schools shared in common, however, was something that had quickly become central to our understanding: time was the one variable that we had control over. What is a master schedule anyway but a way to divide time into effective, manageable blocks that give students what they need to be successful? When expectations are held constant for everyone, time becomes the biggest asset or the most serious barrier in achieving them.

The Professional Gets Personal: My Years as a Mentor

From 1999 to 2003, I "adopted" a group of at-risk freshmen at Lincoln High School and pledged to stay with them for all four years of school. Lincoln's mentor program drew on all kinds of community leaders to do this and it seemed a great opportunity for me to get in touch with our most struggling students. The position meant creating relationships, doing periodic personal mentoring, and providing some special opportunities outside of school. We were each assigned ten students. After some initial training, we were given a series of lessons to guide our first year of mentoring. Then we were on our own.

I remember the first day we met our kids. They came into a designated classroom where we had donuts and juice for them. My palms were sweaty as we greeted these kids—a mixed group of girls and boys, reflective of Lincoln's ethnic diversity. Most of them looked like typical young teenagers: somewhat disheveled, their shoulders slumping, their eyes avoiding prolonged contact with the adults.

It was a tough first meeting. I'm not sure what they had been told, but it seemed obvious that none of them had actually volunteered for this. They seemed wary of us and getting them to talk was like the proverbial "pulling teeth." So we did most of the talking, using our orientation lesson as an opportunity for them to get to know us. We talked about ourselves and why we became mentors. We expressed great hope about their coming four years and promised to be there to help them. We gave them our phone numbers and let them know they could call us if they needed anything at any time. Yet, as hard as we tried to get them to talk about themselves and their aspirations, we learned very little about our kids that day. I left somewhat deflated and unsure of what to expect next.

All ten of them came back the next month. They seemed more upbeat and this time they went right for the snacks. They even talked—well, most of them did. I got the impression that the change was because they were relieved that we had come back. A lifetime of disappointment had probably convinced some of them that we wouldn't show up again.

The first grading period was a disaster. Most of our kids had an abundance of Fs. This was a pattern that repeated itself every six weeks. The year ended with our kids behind the curve in grades and credits, most of them seriously behind. As much as we tried to encourage them and refer them to academic support systems, nothing we did seemed to matter. Nothing except the fact that we didn't go away. We didn't give up on them. We became a constant in their tumultuous lives. We took them to lunch, to the theater, to sporting events and museums. That's one of the most surprising things I learned—how much it means to simply show up.

(continued)

(continued)

Most important, we never stopped letting them know that they had value and were capable of doing whatever they chose. And gradually, they did let us in. Over the years, I learned a lot about their issues outside of school: distressed family situations, siblings and parents in trouble with the law, gang influence, abuse, alcoholism, and drug addiction. They also opened up about their experiences inside school—most of them not so stellar. Relationships with teachers and administrators had been largely negative. The kids had all been in trouble for acting out or skipping classes. Their grades reflected their struggles both inside and outside of school.

Despite our best efforts, we saw only half of our group graduate. It was hard for me to accept my failure to keep all of "my" kids on track, especially because so much of my work was dedicated to this very goal. The personal challenge felt so different from the professional one. But for those students who stuck it out, senior year was a time of immense celebration. I knew I had made a difference for this group because they told me so. I was so proud to shake their hands as they crossed the stage at commencement. We didn't just make formal superintendent–graduating senior eye contact; we shared real hugs and tears. Three out of the five headed for college; they had earned the grades to get them there.

It was incredibly validating to know that the generally poor academic performance of our kids in the early years of high school had nothing to do with ability. Our kids were smart and never complained that school was too hard or that they would be better off in easier classes. Those who stuck it out did better as they progressed into the most rigorous classes and their grades gradually improved. I also understood just how important personal relationships are in connecting our most fragile students to school. I knew it before, but I certainly deepened my understanding as my kids hung in there in spite of their circumstances. Overall, I learned that the journey would always be rough for students on the margin and I rededicated myself to helping build into the system as much support as I could to give them every chance to succeed.

GETTING SERIOUS ABOUT SUMMER SCHOOL

One of the biggest blocks of malleable time available to us was the summer. Summer school in our district had never been much more than a credit-recovery program. Students were rewarded for "seat time," that is, if you came every day and filled your seat, you'd most likely pass. Classes were over-loaded (up to forty-five students in a room). Instructors were chosen not because they were the best or because they cared deeply about students mastering content but simply because they wanted the extra money.

It was time to get serious about summer school, to consider it a real school with expectations of student engagement during class, rules of behavior, homework assignments, and end-of-course tests that counted toward grades. We recruited our most talented teachers and lowered class size from forty to twenty-five.

Over the first few years of our reform efforts, summer school in San Jose underwent a complete reconceptualization. Rather than a punishment for a failing grade, we treated summer school as an opportunity to catch students up in their deficient skills so they could advance to the next level class with a much better chance at success. We recognized that some kids who fail a class don't need to repeat the entire class. If we could identify the deficiencies that led to the failing grade, we could correct them, and let the student recover the credit and move on.

Making these changes on behalf of our students had a fiscal impact, of course. Summer school had always been a cash cow that fed surplus money back into the budget for the regular year, so by not stockpiling as many bodies as possible into a single classroom, we had to plan for that lost revenue. But we did it because it was the right thing to do.

SUMMER BRIDGE

We soon recognized that we had another block of time to make use of: the summer months between eighth and ninth grades. What could we do to help get students on solid footing before they entered high school?

We developed a program called "Summer Bridge." It was conceived as a way to get kids who might already be behind up-to-speed, taught by high school teachers in those district schools that served the largest concentration of struggling students. We implemented this with the first incoming class mandated to take on the new curriculum. We secured a sponsor for the program, Applied Materials, who stepped up to provide funding that simply did not exist in the state budget.

The bridge was specifically designed to transition students who were seriously deficient in core academic skills into high school. We wanted to jumpstart their entry-level coursework in high school, particularly in math, where basic skills often needed to be shored up, and in English, for those struggling readers in need of an intensive boost.

We also recognized the need to offer classes in nonacademic skills, such as note-taking, study habits, and time management. We had learned that teaching these skills to incoming freshmen could push them toward success in their most crucial year of high school.

There was a psychological aspect to Summer Bridge as well. Students who struggle often fear entering high school, and that fear can have an inhibiting effect on academic performance. So we located Summer Bridge on our high school campuses as a way to allow incoming freshmen to get acclimated and comfortable before they were engulfed by the masses, with all the potential pressure that can bring. As a result, the first day of school became a much less frightening and overwhelming milestone for these students.

In setting up Summer Bridge, we recognized that a student's journey through high school begins before he or she arrives. We understood the need for a preventative measure, designed to head off trouble before it took root. From today's vantage point, Summer Bridge has been an effective way to induct students into a challenging high school curriculum and keep them engaged. It may be one of the key reasons that, as standards have risen in San Jose Unified, dropout rates have not.

> Summer Bridge may be one of the key reasons that, as standards have risen in San Jose Unified, dropout rates have not.

CREATING OPPORTUNITIES FOR ACCELERATION

On the other end of the spectrum, many students were indeed ready in eighth grade to take on the high school curriculum. To address the needs of these students, we began to create policies that allowed them to earn high school credit by exam for courses central to the new college-readiness standards, including algebra, geometry, and world languages. Our thinking was that students who could demonstrate mastery by the end of middle school could get a leg up on their core requirements, thereby opening up opportunities for them in higher-level classes—plus more openings in their schedules for electives.

For example, eighth-graders who were ready could take algebra—a class that at the time was credit-based only for high school students. A student who passed could earn high school credit and then go on to geometry in ninth grade, alongside other ninth- and tenth-graders in a high school geometry class.

Like a lot of things we tried, this was a bit of a controversial move. High school math teachers were not easily convinced that algebra taught in middle school was the equivalent of algebra taught in high school. Fair enough. We challenged our district high school math council to write a common end-of-course algebra exam that would measure algebra proficiency and mastery. Students who passed algebra would take the exam to earn high school credit; students who didn't pass didn't get the credit. We used that exam (and similar ones in geometry and world languages) to award high school credit to students in middle school from then on.

In time, I saw that this process had reaped us an extra benefit. It brought middle school and high school math teachers into a working relationship that had never existed before. In our efforts to better serve students, our vision of creating a more holistic district got a nice boost.

Here's another example of how we tried to identify student potential where previously it might have been overlooked: we began requiring that every sophomore take the PSAT (Preliminary Scholarship Aptitude Test). The PSAT signals how well someone will do on the SAT, the exam required by most colleges and universities for admission. Making the PSAT mandatory was a way to give students early feedback on their strengths and weaknesses in terms of college readiness.

The PSAT requirement added a deeper benefit to simple feedback. The College Board has gathered evidence that even students who received poor grades in their core coursework might do well enough on a cluster of PSAT items to indicate that they have potential for success in AP classes (an analysis called AP Potential). This seemed like data that we could exploit to help out students who might have considered AP out of their reach. Because we had decided to set up open enrollment in AP courses as a way of giving opportunity to all students, we wanted to pull more of them, particularly under-represented minorities, into these higher-level classes. Looking over the AP Potential report became a way for us to predict success for kids whose mediocre grades might previously have left them overlooked by teachers who wouldn't think to push them toward AP classes.

In summary, now that we had a better understanding of our students' high school journeys, we began to find all sorts of ways to transform the path into something more beneficial. It was an exciting time in our district. Our belief and our vision were being rewarded. Our students were responding to the challenge.

STUDENTS WITH SPECIAL NEEDS AND ENGLISH LANGUAGE LEARNERS

Under a more rigorous curriculum, certain students will inevitably require more attention than others. In San Jose, we were able to envision a way that most of our students, with appropriate support, would have full access to the college- and career-preparatory course work and the potential for real success. But we knew from the start there would be subsets of the student population—such as some special needs students and some English language learners (ELL)—who would need individualized learning paths. For these students, requirements could be modified on a case-by-case basis:

- Modified graduation pathways were created for some special needs students through the individual education plan (IEP) process.
- English language acquisition was made the first priority for ELL students, many of whom were often newcomers to the United States and had very limited literacy skills. Although many English language learners can and do complete the college and career course requirements, those who are under extreme hardship (for example, recent immigrants who had limited schooling in their home country) were provided a modified pathway (individual learning plan) to graduation according to their needs.

REACHING THE OUTLIERS: SAFETY NETS AND SUPPORTS

For all our efforts, no matter how comprehensive, we recognized that there would continue to be outliers, the 10 percent of students who cannot make it in a traditional comprehensive high school. These are the students who are in real danger of dropping out and need a much more personalized learning environment to graduate high school.

For these outliers, the curriculum needs to be modified as well. These students are often dealing with serious personal and family problems; they don't fit in; and they desperately need personal attention and closer relationships with adults in order to build their self-esteem and persevere through high school. Among the larger population, they're a relatively small group, but you can't let them fumble and fail. You have to provide a different kind of path through high school.

These students' frequent failures often are due to the fact that they just don't show up. They may not formally drop out, but they stop engaging, and by the time they reach junior year, they often have only freshman-level credits. We paid a lot of attention to these outliers in the early stages of our reforms, trying to create greater safety nets where there had been only scattershot programs before. All of these programs were small and focused and based on an intervention model:

- We established a school at our regional occupational training center so that some students were able to pursue career-technical pathways while taking their academic classes on site.

- We strengthened our continuation high school program and brought in technology to enhance learning opportunities.

- We partnered with a local hospital to begin a career academy on site. Students got experience working at the hospital while also taking all of their academic classes there. And they were paid for it. We assigned a single teacher for all classes, creating a very personalized learning environment.

- We instituted very small alternative schools at each high school. These schools had two teachers and a counselor responsible for forty students who had fallen seriously behind and who needed an individualized learning plan to guide their advancement.

- We expanded our middle-college program at a local community college, allowing students to attend school there full time with the opportunity to earn both high school and college credit. This was a good fit for high school students who learned better in an adult environment.

- We expanded independent study options for students with severe credit deficiencies.

College and career graduation requirements were never intended to be a magic wand that could magically rescue this 10 percent, but we made it our business to ensure that our reforms took the situation of our most at-risk students seriously. Guided by attentive teachers and counselors who were given as much support as possible to help these outlier students, we were able to understand, and change for the better, what had previously been a very perilous journey through high school for these students. It's one of the most important things we did.

Shoring Up the Pipeline

So what did we do about the fact that many students were at a disadvantage when entering high school? Much of our work was focused on shoring up the pipeline—getting kids up to speed going all the way back to kindergarten:

- We brought in research-based reading programs, such as Success for All, to boost reading levels of our below-grade-level students. We invested in Reading Recovery for those most at risk.

- We gave young children enriched summer school opportunities using computer-based programs, such as Voyager, which engaged students and greatly improved literacy skills.

- We placed math and language arts literacy coaches in our elementary schools to work daily with teachers.

- We challenged our curriculum councils in math, language arts, and science to backward-map the standards that would lead to proficiency with respect to the new exit requirements.

- We focused on early transition for English learners, with an expectation that those who started with us in kindergarten

---

would be fully English proficient prior to exiting elementary school. At the same time, we expanded two-way immersion programs through eighth grade to promote full fluency in English and Spanish.

- In middle school, we did away with all tracking and redesigned the core curriculum to prepare all students for a rigorous high school experience.
- Remedial and advanced classes disappeared in middle school. Heterogeneous grouping in English, social studies, and science gave all students exposure to the same content at the same high levels.
- In middle school math, the basic prealgebra content was the same for all students, but we introduced algebra and geometry for students who had mastered the basic curricula.
- World languages were also introduced in middle school as electives for those who expressed interest.

In many cases, the safety nets and supports that we set up for struggling high school students—such as homework centers, tutoring, and extended-day opportunities—were implemented in the early grades, too. Philosophically we believed that just-in-time interventions must be in place to catch children up and accelerate their learning. The old-school notion of "remedial education" was holding way too many students back and in fact creating larger and larger achievement gaps as children progressed through their early years. For many children, our shift in thinking and the programs we put into place from the early grades on made a huge difference down the line.

BRICKS, MORTAR, AND SCIENCE LABS

There's no way to talk about the students' journey through high school without talking about the school itself—the actual buildings, classrooms, and facilities in which learning takes place. When we instituted college- and career-ready graduation requirements, we increased the pressure on our physical infrastructure. Now that we had decided all students would take lab science in order to graduate, we had to ask ourselves, Did we have enough science labs to support them? The answer came quickly: we definitely did not.

We were now faced with a whole new set of charts in our war room, this time taking stock of the physical reality of our facilities:

- How many labs would be needed?

- What was our current inventory, high school by high school?

- Were they up-to-date enough to accommodate lab needs?

- Where would we find enough labs to make up the difference?

- How would we pay for the expensive new facilities that would be needed to give every student access?

- Were there stop-gap measures that would mitigate our needs or technology solutions that could make lab experiences accessible online?

These questions were of highest priority as we planned to phase in our curriculum reforms. But to some degree, we were getting ahead of ourselves because the state of *all* our facilities was so poor that there were greater needs than labs that first had to be addressed. Many of the district's schools were built over sixty years previously, and little had been done to upgrade them or take care of routine maintenance.

When I got to San Jose, our facilities were atrocious: old, decrepit, poorly maintained, and often not up to safety standards. When I'd visit schools, I was embarrassed by what I saw—embarrassed that we were asking students to put up with such conditions. A rainstorm the night before might mean a teacher had to rearrange her class on one side of the room because the other was wet from a leaky wall. Water damage destroyed computers; floors got torn up and remained unfixed. Our heating would break down all the time in the winter, shutting schools in the middle of the day when many of our smallest children had nowhere to go. (We'd take them to a high school and put them in a gym.)

There are very few state funds to help with these kinds of problems. Revenue needs to be raised locally through bonds. It had been a long time since anyone had passed a bond measure in Santa Clara County, but, knowing what we needed to do, we launched a campaign. We started with a poll, in 1994, to test the tolerance of the voters. We were estimating a need of $500 to $600 million, but our poll revealed voter tolerance at around $160 million. So we drafted a first measure that would pay for renovation, remodeling, and repair of serious structural problems such as inadequate plumbing.

Our wish for upgrading science facilities went to the back burner, delayed but not derailed. We put the focus on student safety and welfare concerns and we ran a winning campaign. We talked to a lot of residents. We walked the streets. We distributed pictures of the decay in our schools so that the voters could see the horrible conditions that surrounded our community's young people every day.

That bond passed with over 70 percent support. It gave us a great boost, not only financially but also in terms of morale. We felt that we had a real chance to earn back the public trust. We went right to work, putting the money into schools as allocated, wanting to give the people what they voted for and the students what they deserved—a safe, functioning environment.

The first bond measure allowed us to direct a small portion of the funds into renovation of lab facilities, though not for real modernization and certainly not for brand-new facilities, which is what we really needed. It fell on us as leaders to map out a plan to create enough stations to give all students access to lab work. (Ideally, there would be one student at every lab station, but when we began, we were happy to have enough stools for them all to sit on. Squeezing two or three to a single station was sometimes necessary.)

In our effort to teach lab science to all high school students, we had to try a little bit of everything to make it happen:

- We played with the master schedule and began scheduling labs in the early-morning zero period, as well as in an after-school seventh period, so that labs could be used for up to eight periods a day rather than the traditional six.

- We began to open labs on Saturdays so that students could meet lab requirements on weekends.

- We developed partnerships with our local community colleges, allowing some students to dual-enroll and meet their science requirements there. In other cases, science labs at community colleges would be made available for K–12 science teachers to use on a scheduled basis.

A long-range solution required a new influx of public funding. A few years later, we went back to the voters. Even though the second bond was considerably larger ($400 million), it too passed. We now had the resources to modernize and add science facilities. It was a plan that stretched out over many years and included the creation not just of stations and classrooms but also entire science buildings. We wanted state-of-the-art facilities, and we determined that money could be saved on infrastructure by centralizing several of the high schools' lab needs into a single building.

Today, all of San Jose's high schools have modernized their science facilities and offer adequate stations for all students. In 2008, the last building was dedicated, fourteen years after we first prioritized the need.

Similar to providing safety nets for the outlying 10 percent of struggling students, upgrading our bricks and mortar seemed, at the start, like a nearly insurmountable task. We learned a lesson in San Jose about the absolute necessity of short-term solutions that built toward long-term progress— to say nothing of the patience and perseverance necessary for success.

READER REFLECTION

1. What were the most important things the district did to implement the reform agenda around college and career readiness for all?

2. Can you think of other important initiatives a district might pursue to make this reform successful? Describe them.

CHAPTER FOUR

Teachers

A Force to Reckon With

"You can do it!"

The power of the words, "You can do it!" and the belief behind them were brought home to me by one San Jose student, a senior who had just graduated under the new college- and career-ready requirements fully eligible for UC admissions. He said, "Hearing someone tell you 'You can do it!' makes you think: 'She thinks I can, so I must be able to.'" He was talking about his teachers, about their commitment to his education.

Your teaching force is just that, a *force*—probably the most powerful one you have at your disposal. One of the biggest challenges you're going to face in the process of delivering a more rigorous curriculum is how to maximize that force.

We can all do the math. More rigorous requirements plus more interventions means more teachers in the academic core. Back when we started our reforms in San Jose, we knew we'd be stretched and we knew we would face a gap in teacher capacity. We knew we had eighteen hundred teachers in our district. What we didn't have was a clear picture of the depth and breadth of their talents. We committed the time and the energy to find out. Our human resources staff poured through hundreds of individual personnel files one at a time, by hand, to give us a more complete picture. We began by asking every relevant question we could think of:

- Who held what credentials?
- Who was teaching something other than what was needed in our new generation of high schools?
- Did these teachers hold other credentials that would allow them to be redeployed in areas of critical need?
- Were there elementary and middle school teachers who might teach math, science, and world languages in high school?
- How old was our workforce? Whom would we lose to retirement? Whom would we have to replace just to stay even?

We began tying our transcript data—grades and course-taking patterns—to our deployment of faculty. Looking at math and sciences, for example, the first thing we considered was how much talent was wasted by teachers reteaching courses because of high failure rates. Could we mitigate the need to hire new teachers by getting students through these classes the first time they took them?

We had already begun eliminating low-level courses such as general math, consumer math, and prealgebra from the high school curriculum. Now we asked ourselves, if we eliminate all of the low-level courses, and if we could, by design, cut failure rates in half, would that allow our teacher talent be redeployed into expanded algebra, geometry, and algebra II classes—the more rigorous offerings necessary for students to meet college entrance requirements? Similarly, could we redeploy teachers teaching courses such as life science and physical science into biology, chemistry, or physics?

For world languages, we faced the problem that vast numbers of students had been taking none at all, so we had a serious shortage of qualified teachers. Further complicating this was the fact that some teachers in our district held a world language credential but were teaching younger students enrolled in bilingual education programs. Could we entice some of these teachers into teaching world language courses and how would we then backfill for the needs of bilingual students? Where would we find the added teachers to fill this major gap?

Another component of this analysis was to look at teachers close to retirement, many of whom were teaching courses that would no longer be offered under our new graduation plan. A notable number of these senior teachers were outspoken critics of the idea that all students could be prepared successfully for college. They weren't bad teachers, but they openly opposed our reform plan.

It was at this point that I approached the teachers' union to look at options for exiting these veterans in a way that honored their service but gave them an incentive to retire. As I've already discussed in Chapter Two, the savings in salary from veteran to replacement teachers was substantial and funded the retirement package with enough savings left over to increase significantly the starting salary for our replacement teachers. That made recruitment easier in the competitive marketplace. Everyone benefited in the end.

Making all of these determinations was not an exact science by any means, and though we developed many fresh solutions, our thinking often wasn't linear. Yours won't be either. In the next chapters that cover the audit and blueprint step-by-step, the question of how to determine your teacher needs will be raised again. You should read these chapters with an eye toward adapting this linear presentation of our model to the situations and opportunities presented within your own district.

To be perfectly frank, there was an aspect of calculated risk to our strategizing. Driven by a sense of where we wanted to end up, we began putting pieces of the puzzle together. We were able to make reasonable assumptions from the data we had, and we began to create a gap analysis that seemed defensible to us. We ended this critically important analysis of our teaching capacity in an optimistic mood. With aggressive recruitment and a strong professional development plan, it seemed possible to meet the instructional demands of a college- and career-preparatory course of study for all students.

FINDING THE TEACHERS WE NEEDED

We had four years to phase in the full complement of teachers required so recruitment and hiring could be rolled out as students progressed through the new curriculum from ninth to twelfth grade. With this in mind, our plan incorporated several tactics.

San Jose Unified was already recruiting from colleges nationwide; now we recalibrated our plan toward institutions that produced large numbers of math and science teachers. To find world language teachers, we expanded our recruitment to the international marketplace, including Spain, Mexico, and Central and South America. We also got a lot of help through the Visiting International Faculty program, a state-endorsed effort that brings qualified instructors to the United States on three-year teaching visas.

Knowing that people skilled in math and science were likely to be found working professionally in their fields, we began a partnership with the New Teacher Project (NTP), an East Coast nonprofit organization dedicated in part to recruiting individuals from industry—often people who are at mid-career and itchy for a change—into the teaching profession. San Jose's location in the Silicon Valley left us in close proximity to an abundance of talent.

We also benefited at this time from a sudden downturn in the economy. In 2000, the first wave of Internet optimism was "correcting" itself, leading to what became known as the dot-com bust. At the very time we needed to deepen our recruiting and hiring, there were suddenly a lot of very talented people looking for jobs. A lot of these folks were in their early to mid-thirties—young, energetic, and looking for the next challenge. Many of them had previously thought about teaching but had instead been drawn into more lucrative careers. Now, stock options from their dot-com jobs cashed in, they were once again available.

The NTP screened applicants, helped us hire the ones we needed, and implemented an internship program that ended with certification. It was a very structured approach, modeled after Teach for America, and very successful for San Jose. Over two hundred teachers came to the district in the two years the NTP worked with us. Some of them already lived here and owned their homes, which augured a certain amount of stability.

These professionals had extensive knowledge, though by and large they didn't know how to teach. A lot of these folks came in thinking, rather naively, "I know the material; how hard can it be?" But what they lacked was experience in how to manage a classroom, how to pace instruction, how to transmit knowledge to a room full of teenagers, and so on. Some of them, having always worked with adults, took it for granted that when you talk, people listen. It was a rude awakening to discover that getting students to listen required a new set of skills or a new kind of effort. Some of these teachers washed out in the first year. Overall, however, attrition was no greater than for first-year teachers out of traditional teacher-preparation programs, and these candidates were much more apt to have solid subject-area competence. Their experience in the field meant that they could explain how the skills they were teaching could be applied in the real world, and students responded to that. Enough of this group stuck with it to make a big difference to us.

Circumstances certainly worked in our favor here, but it would be incorrect to simply chalk all of this up to coincidence, luck, or fate. In my opinion, it was unabashed opportunism. We were, as far as I know, the only California district that pursued the New Teacher Project at this critical historical moment. Through our many long meetings, we refused to see the problem of teacher recruitment as insurmountable, and so when we saw a window of opportunity, we didn't waste any time. People out of jobs possessed the talent we were looking for. We could teach them to be the teachers we needed. We took advantage of the moment. That's the lesson here.

> "I was seldom able to see an opportunity until it had ceased to be one . . ."—Mark Twain

---

Opportunism: A Necessary Component of Leadership

For me, a vital part of leadership is the capacity to leap at whatever comes up, whenever it comes up—because opportunity rarely knocks twice.

The educational system is populated by folks who believe in following rules. That's a good thing—except that what tends to happen is that daring gets smoked out and silenced. Don't get the parents upset; keep the teachers' union at bay; don't push bold, untested ideas. Although caution can be useful, too much of it means that the same old assumptions become intractable, locking everything into stasis, with no room for smart risk-taking.

The danger with playing it safe or being too risk averse is that you don't go for it when the chance is there. When I think of milestone moments that allowed A–G For All to take root and grow, I think of the way we made the most of Silicon Valley going bust—by aggressively recruiting pink-slipped dot-com workers into the classroom. That kind of step had to happen with immediacy. We leapt into risk. It was an opportunistic thing to do—but it paid off quickly.

TEACHING THE TEACHERS: PROFESSIONAL DEVELOPMENT THAT WORKS

All studies show that nothing makes a difference to a student like a good teacher, and a great teacher inevitably makes a great difference. But how do teachers become great? The teaching experience can be an isolating one, especially in high school when teachers are separated from each other by discipline. An English teacher may not know a math teacher at all, though they may both be challenged by the same students.

If you interviewed a roomful of teachers anywhere in the United States, they would say that most professional development aimed at them is wasted. We heard plenty from teachers in focus groups and other venues about most efforts being really just "drive-by development," one-day workshops that they "pick out of a binder." These workshops might offer a helpful idea or two, but they almost never include an opportunity to try out those ideas in a substantial way. Workshops need follow-up if their lessons are going to stick.

In San Jose, our teachers had become disillusioned with the very idea of professional development because it was hard to see any real effect on instructional practices and student outcomes. The best intentions and plans got shelved. So we had to rethink our entire approach to professional development—how we were spending our resources and how we were delivering on them.

We became much more open to listening to what teachers said they needed, something that began in those original focus groups when we were first exploring with teachers the possibilities of engaging all students in a college- and career-preparatory course of study. Teachers told us that they would need extra support to reach students who were being held up to higher standards and being pushed further than ever before. Teachers wanted to be successful; they didn't want to see their students fail. Indeed, they considered this their professional and ethical responsibility.

Both new and veteran instructors told us they wanted training that followed something along the lines of a clinical model—the way interns learn from doctors in hospitals—in which they could pick up new techniques, try them out in the classroom, and take the time to reflect on outcomes with other teachers. They wanted to hone their skills by making use of the best practices in the field, and they wanted to apply these in the classroom with students. The idea of having other teachers observing them in a nonevaluative, growth-oriented way was very appealing. This kind of embedded development would not only benefit students, it would also allow for relationships among teachers along the lines of old-fashioned mentorships.

In San Jose, we started to figure out how to drive professional development into the schools rather than send teachers off-campus to expensive, one-day workshops. To the extent that this was possible, we began to shift our professional development dollars, giving a lot of control to site administrators and their teachers to choose what they wanted to do with them.

We had a good model already in place. In the early 1990s, we had implemented a beginning teacher support and assessment program (BTSA). Brand-new teachers went through an induction period during their first two critical years before tenure, mentored by a master teacher. This was an intense, formative evaluation process. Finding the resources—and the time—to conduct quality professional development such as BTSA for all teachers was a huge challenge, but we made a good start.

Chief among our efforts was the creation of teaching coaches. These coaches were given periods off from teaching to work with colleagues on content and pedagogical skills. In addition, teachers themselves began to generate the topics in which they felt they needed training and coaching. Among the things we heard about were the following:

- *Differentiated instruction.* How do you teach algebra to a classroom that might include students who have poor basic computational skills? With students now in heterogeneous groupings rather than tracked by perceived ability, instructors needed new skills and strategies, such as project-based learning, to reach all students at the same time in the same room.

- *Cultural competence.* Students of different backgrounds relate differently to instruction in the classroom. Helping teachers understand this kind of cultural diversity in a nuanced way and cultivating respect for what each student brings into a classroom was something we knew would improve access to college and career coursework for all students.

- *Use of data to drive instruction.* Just because we had accumulated a lot of data didn't mean that they were always accessible to teachers. Guiding teachers toward making good use of data, teaching them how to generate useful reports on a regular basis, and encouraging data review with their colleagues was a natural area for professional development. Today in San Jose teachers work in data teams and visit each other for necessary information based on the success of this effort (see Chapter Nine). Other topics included standards-based grading practices, deconstructing standards, scaffolding techniques, and professional collaboration around best practices and effective use of technology.

Our state funded five days per year of professional development, but that was simply not enough. Teachers yearned for time to collaborate and learn new strategies to augment student success.

As with so many aspects of our reform efforts, the key here was time. If you're teaching five classes a day, where do you find the time for professional development? This was where the district could step in and free up time—especially the time of our master teachers, who might take on that coach-mentor role. Schools were encouraged to create common planning periods whenever possible so that teachers in the same subject areas would have daily time together and be less isolated during this time of change. We encouraged shortened instructional days on a weekly basis, which meant adding minutes to other days, so that teachers would have time to collaborate with one another and engage in on-site professional development.

Teachers were learning to increase their expectations of students, and the district was learning to increase our expectations of teachers. We had to believe in the teachers and support them when they were clearly asking for guidance and resources. It wasn't always easy, but it was absolutely necessary.

ACCOUNTABILITY WITH COLLABORATION

For me, one of the most powerful aspects of watching our high schools evolve was that this evolution was a joint effort by district and site leaders. Though the central office created opportunities across high schools, whenever appropriate, each school had to come up with its own plan to make sure all students had access to a rigorous curriculum and no student fell through the cracks without an intervention. That these schools were accountable for the plans they enacted meant that much was on the line. Everyone took it seriously.

"Accountability" can sound like a punitive thing, but in this case, school accountability to the district and district accountability to our schools felt like a true collaboration. Each of our six high schools reported to the board of education once a year at a public meeting. These meetings were a chance to let everyone know about the programs that had been put into place and to share data showing their successes and challenges. The board asked many questions, but the tone was one of appreciation rather than interrogation. We all understood the importance of acknowledging the hard work being done, the effort everyone was putting into making our students more successful.

Best of all, these presentations meant that our board meetings got to focus purely on curriculum—a breath of fresh air in a venue that was often heavy with procedure and bureaucracy.

At these meetings, a school's principal and leadership team (assistant principals, key instructors, and students) were given an hour to tell the stories of all that they were doing to make A–G work for the students. Administrators would talk to the board about their leadership in driving instructional change. Teachers would speak about success stories and struggles, using data to back up their presentations. Students talked about what it meant to them to be challenged to high standards. As time went on, the presenters got more elaborate, employing PowerPoint or passing out samples of student work. Leaders from different schools would attend each others' presentations as a way to prepare for their own moments in the spotlight. The meetings came to serve as a kind of professional development. I always looked forward to these nights. In the midst of a lot of hard work, they were a chance to step back and celebrate results.

One-on-One with Principals

It's hard to get a superintendent's undivided attention, but I made it a priority to give mine to my principals. Each year I met with every district principal—forty-two of them. Time-consuming, yes, but also invaluable. We called these meetings our "one-on-ones." They weren't top-down, threatening meetings; my principals looked forward to them. Like most people in positions of responsibility, they wanted to know for what they were accountable.

Before each meeting, my data guru would print out a one-page sheet on the past performance of students in the school. We'd use that as a starting point. We looked at low scores and talked about what would be done about them, including what was needed from me and from the district to get there. Each school had its own particular issues that focused our meetings. We might look at the number of suspensions and strategize how that rate would be cut in one year's time. They didn't always

(continued)

(continued)
meet their targets, but they always took the steps that they'd promised to make.

Strong principals create good relationships with their faculties. They set goals with their teachers and lead them toward improvement. Strong principals are in classrooms with their teachers; they're instructional leaders as well as managers and they're not apt to let poor teachers slide by. They walk the halls, staying visible, so that kids know who they are. They are diligent in making sure students get what they need.

RESULTS FIRST

Today, professional development in the San Jose Unified School District has become largely teacher driven. This took time. Significantly, it also took *results* before anything really gained momentum.

The "elephant in the room" in terms of professional development revolved around teachers' expectations. Many of them just didn't expect students to benefit from rigorous academics. We thought long and hard about how to instill the belief that all students *can* truly be successful in a college-preparatory curriculum. Was there a way to do this through professional development? We certainly tried, in the early years of our efforts, to do just that. We brought in motivational speakers, held districtwide diversity trainings, publicized data that exposed achievement gaps in inarguable ways, and created accountability systems that publicly reported on achievement and opportunity gaps. But we found that none of these completely convinced teachers.

No, the way to change attitudes and beliefs was through demonstrable results. When teachers saw students who had never been able to master difficult material now succeed in their classes, expectations finally began to change.

I don't believe we change the hearts and minds of teachers until they experience success with those they traditionally expect to fail—those students who would otherwise continue to be relegated to a low-level curriculum and a worthless diploma. Until that happens, however, you have to demand, one way or another, that teachers teach all students at a high level and teach them well. You must insist of them: teach every child the way you would want your own children to be taught.

> " . . . When teachers ask students to do work that seems 'too hard,' they are often surprised to find that students can do it. In these cases, adult beliefs about what children can learn are changed by watching students do things that the adults didn't believe that they—the students—could do."— Richard Elmore, "I Used to Think . . . and Now I Think . . . ", *Harvard Education Letter*, 26, no. 1 (January/February 2010).

For me, this comes back to that idea that a leader has to set a stake in the sand. Start with the mandate for change and then do the necessary work. High expectations for all will follow when you have the results to show for it.

READER REFLECTION

1. How important is it to involve teachers in determining what kind of professional development they need and how it is delivered? Discuss. What are the most important things that districts and schools should do to get teachers and administrators committed to the equity agenda?

2. Do you think opportunism and risk taking are critical aspects of school reform? Explain.

CHAPTER FIVE

The Educational Opportunity Audit

"My mom and dad didn't finish high school. My proudest accomplishment is that I will graduate and go on to college."

—African American student, 2008

It's time to get down to the nitty-gritty. My idea in writing this book is to empower you to implement college- and career-ready reforms in your own district. The toolkit in this and the next chapter will help get you there. Though some of these tools might seem useful individually, they are meant to work comprehensively. I don't recommend doing this kind of systematic overhaul in a piecemeal way.

Remember, you can visit our Web site, www .edtrustwest.org, at any time to download templates, protocols, surveys and other supporting material.

HOW LONG WILL IT TAKE?

From district to district, the amount of time it takes to complete the educational opportunity audit and blueprint will vary, though a range of one to one and a half years is a good estimate. At the end of Chapter Six, you'll find a sample timeline that will give you an idea of how this breaks out, step by step.

START BY DEFINING YOUR REQUIREMENTS

Step one in this process is to align your high school graduation requirements with your state's college and university entrance requirements. As of now, no national high school curriculum standards exist in the United States (although the common standards movement may get us there eventually). Each and every state is unique. In California, rather than having each public university decide what specific courses a student must take at a minimum to apply for entry, our state university system has created the A–G requirements (see Chapter One) to make this determination. In other states, the National Collegiate Athletic Association (NCAA) requirements serve as a guideline.

Before you can proceed, you'll need to agree up front what your district considers college preparatory. Everything else follows from there.

GATHERING YOUR TEAM

Who does the work? Someone has to lead your district through the educational opportunity audit and that person is mostly likely going to be the superintendent. Conceivably the superintendent might assign a high-level leadership group to take on the work. This leadership group would most likely include assistant superintendents and other high-ranking officials who report directly to the superintendent. These leaders will guide the crucial early legwork, such as gathering artifacts and statewide data.

From there, you will assemble a larger data team. They will be crucial when transcript analysis is undertaken. This team's primary goal is to uncover barriers that students come up against as they progress through high school. As the name implies, the data team must be made up of key personnel who are "data savvy."

The data team should include people from the following disciplines:

- Central office leaders for
    - Instruction
    - Human resources
    - Finance
    - Facilities
- Key staff members who specialize in
    - Curriculum
    - Professional development
    - Student support services
    - Special education
    - English language learning
    - Alternative education
    - Student assessment
    - Information services
- Site leaders such as
    - Principals and assistant principals from each middle and high school
    - Teachers from each middle and high school across the major disciplines
    - Counselors from each high school

- Registrars from each high school
- At least one elementary school representative

GATHERING YOUR MATERIALS

What do you need to get started? The first step of the educational opportunity audit is looking at where your district is now. Your leadership group will collect and study a series of relevant artifacts—transcripts, achievement data, the master schedule, and so on, charting where the district currently is in providing all students with a rigorous and relevant education. Examining these artifacts will help you determine:

- The level of preparation of most recent graduates
- Gaps among significant subgroups in student participation in rigorous courses
- District policies and practices that impede students from accessing rigorous courses
- Choke points where students most often opt out of higher-level classes
- Available interventions

Artifacts to Be Gathered for the Educational Opportunity Audit

1. Senior transcripts of the most recent graduating class. In addition to standard transcript information, transcripts *must* be augmented to indicate the following:
   - Student ethnicity
   - Special needs programs (special education, English language learners [ELL], migrant education, and so on)
   - Student achievement data and state scores
   - Exit exam results (if applicable, include score and date passed)
   - ELL testing
   - AP scores
   - SAT scores

2. Middle school transcripts or eighth-grade report cards for the recent graduates you are studying

3. Latest achievement data (standardized test results):

   - Districtwide results in the aggregate and broken out by high school, subgroups, and grade level when possible

   - Applicable test data for special needs and ELL students

   - Percentages of special education and ELL (note dominant home language) population at the high school level. Include all available, applicable test data required by state and district.

4. Course catalog for the school and district:

   - Review the course catalogs available in each school or district.

   - Review all prerequisite information.

   - Review graduation requirements—match and compare to statewide college-preparatory requirements.

5. Master calendar:

   - A calendar that denotes all events scheduled during school hours (last year's calendar is acceptable)

6. Current graduation requirements:

   - Requirements for high schools—include credit requirements for any alternative or continuation schools

7. Course guide or student handbook for each high school:

   - Course descriptions and codes for college-preparatory and general classes

   - Course descriptions and codes for special education and ELL classes

   - Course descriptions for electives, vocational, and career-technical education classes

   - Course descriptions for alternative and continuation high schools

8. Master schedule for each high school:

   - Teacher, subject, and class for each period

   - List of courses meeting college-readiness requirements

9. Class load analysis for each high school:

   - Include breakdown of number of students per grade level by teacher and by ethnic group; electronic format preferred, for example, Excel spreadsheet.

10. Bell schedules:

    - The regular bell schedule
    - The minimum day bell schedule and any special schedules for each school

11. Testing date information:

    - List by school of the number of days and hours allotted to testing (for example, statewide, benchmark, and final exams)

12. Teacher credential information:

    - List of teachers by school, including their:
      - Subject teaching
      - Areas of credential
      - Years of teaching experience (in and outside of the district)

13. Safety net and curricular-intervention programs:

    - List of programs by high school and approximate number of students serviced, average length of intervention, how students are identified, and any benchmark assessments used with these programs

COLLECTING ACHIEVEMENT TEST DATA

Begin by taking a snapshot of student achievement in your district, focusing on achievement test data that let you compare your district to statewide results. This will help you uncover trends within the district—including the performance of students from different ethnic and socio-economic subgroups—which deepens your understanding of your students' educational experiences. Which subgroups are doing well and which need more support? Disaggregating publicly available data by ethnicity will give you clear insight into the achievement levels of all significant subgroups.

Analyzing this data is critical—this step is where you'll get the first glimpse of the problems in your district. If there's an achievement gap, it will most likely show up here first.

> This is publicly available data; the California Department of Education puts statewide data on a site called Data Quest and many states have an equivalent (though with varying levels of user-friendliness).

TRANSCRIPT STUDY

The study of student transcripts is a powerful way to examine the shortcomings of high school preparation for large segments of the population and clearly understand what the barriers to college and career readiness are.

Discovering Patterns in Your District

In my work with districts throughout California, the study of transcripts is the most eye-opening part of the educational opportunity audit. I suspect you will find this to be true for your analysis as well. No step in this entire process will likely give you as much clarity as the transcript study. By looking at senior transcripts for the last graduating class, you will determine how far the district is from the goal of graduating all students college and career ready.

A Representative Sample

Under the direction of your leadership group, the transcripts of your most recent graduating class must be examined with the intent to cull a representative sample that exposes the following:

- Course-taking patterns in general as well as specific gaps faced by each subgroup
- Common choke points where students begin experiencing failure and opt out of higher level classes. (A choke point is defined as any barrier, whether a course, test, or other hurdle, that prevents students from meeting the statewide college-entry requirements.)
- Unusual or illogical course sequences

- Interventions for struggling students, including support classes and other specialized services

- Standardized test data and exit exam data (if available), to be compared with grades earned in courses

Bringing in the Data Team

Your sample of representative transcripts now goes before the larger data team, who will look closely at this sample to discover how student transcripts reveal patterns among students and core issues for the district. The key question here is, What does a student's current journey through high school look like?

The data team will answer the following questions:

- Do students who start on a college track tend to stay there and get the support they need to be successful?

- If they struggle, are they dropped down to a general track?

- Are students who do well in a general track early in high school challenged to take more rigorous coursework as they progress?

- Are opportunities for timely intervention built into students' schedules? Or is the intervention for students who fail to repeat the same class?

- What academic disciplines pose the biggest barriers to students becoming well prepared for college and good careers?

- Are extra classes provided to help students who are struggling?

- Are career pathways obvious for students who are not pursuing a college track?

- Is the four-year schedule optimizing each student's ability to take academic and elective courses?

- Do students carry a full schedule in senior year? Do English language learners and special needs students have access to college-preparatory classes?

Transcript Study Flow Chart

The leadership group analyzes all transcripts of the most recent graduating class to gain a deep understanding of course-taking patterns, choke points, and interventions. They then draw a representative sample for further study. The steps in this process are as follows:

1. Review all transcripts for the most recent graduating class in the district.

2. Analyze transcripts for course-taking patterns:
   - Determine English, math, science, and world language sequence.
   - Determine college eligibility.
   - Note overall patterns.
   - Identify choke points.
   - Note interventions.
   - Enter all of this into a spreadsheet or database.

3. Select 100 to 150 transcripts:
   - Select a representative, not a random, sample.
   - Choose a proportional sample according to student pathways, ethnicity, and other significant categories.
   - Ensure complete transcripts are in the sample.

4. Gather all nontranscript data for the chosen sample:
   - Ethnicity
   - Test scores
   - Special program status

5. Remove anomalies:
   - Discard those with data holes.
   - Choose the best sample of patterns, choke points, and interventions.

The next step is for the data team to meet with the leadership group to analyze the representative sample of transcripts. The steps in this process are as follows:

1. Examine the leadership group's representative sample for the following:
   - Sequence of courses taken
   - Differences in course-taking by subgroup

- Academic preparation for postsecondary options

- Career-technical pathways

- Relationship between student course grades and achievement on state and district standards assessments

2. Consider what interventions exist to support students. Are others needed?

   - Who gets them?

   - Are they working?

   - Are interventions noted on transcript? Which aren't?

   - Are they timely?

3. Where are the choke points?

   - Do large numbers of students fail a particular course(s)?

   - Do students pursue lower-level courses as a result?

   - Do students reenroll in the same class multiple times?

   - Do students enter remediation or support courses and get stuck?

4. What other factors come into play?

   - Do students and their families have clear information regarding course selection and sequencing, supports, and implications for pursuing certain courses?

   - Are there courses on transcripts not noted in course catalog?

   - Are graduation requirements in each discipline positioning students to access all postsecondary options?

   - Are any important data missing from the transcript?

MASTER SCHEDULE ANALYSIS

The review of the master schedule shines a spotlight on how schools are organized around the instructional program they provide.

Putting the Needs of Students First

You cannot underestimate the importance of the master schedule. Ideally, your schools' administrators and their staff make decisions concerning school-site organization based first and foremost on the needs of the students. However, when we reviewed master schedules in San Jose—along with other materials such as master calendars, bell schedules, class loads, and student handbooks—we discovered that quite often the desires of adults were prioritized over the needs of students. Your data team will examine master schedules from each high school to determine the following.

Use of Instructional Time

Determine the number of regular bell schedule days, the days set aside for testing, any special days such as assemblies and rallies, and any other unique schedules the school adopts.

Next, analyze each school's bell schedule to ascertain the actual number of instructional minutes students receive. Most states require a minimum number of minutes students must attend school. In California, high school students must be in school for 64,800 minutes. Although schools must officially meet this requirement, it's important to analyze how much time students actually get per subject. This analysis takes into account announcements, attendance, clean-up time, and any other factor that reduces the amount of instruction that takes place during any given period. Because it offers more concentrated, uninterrupted instructional time, many schools are choosing a block schedule in place of the traditional high school schedule.

64,800

Number of instructional minutes in a high school year

Analyzing your master schedule in minutes helps determine how much time students get per subject.

School Organization

Now evaluate the actual structure of the master schedule. Be on the lookout for a variety of factors that will aid in determining if your district is offering enough courses to help students meet college-prep requirements. These factors include the following:

- Class sizes
- Teacher assignments
- Course conflicts

- The number of college-prep courses
- The number of advanced courses
- The number and type of support and intervention courses
- The number and type of special education and English language learner courses

For your district, count each course in each subject area—social studies, English, math, science, world languages, fine and performing arts, and other electives—to determine whether it can be considered as meeting college-prep requirements. Then calculate the *percentage* of courses in each subject area deemed college prep. Typically, schools that place a priority on preparing all students for college and career have at least 85 percent of the total number of courses (excluding physical education) meeting college-admission requirements. Similarly, the two areas with the lowest percentage of college-preparatory courses are typically English and math—usually the result of low expectations and tracking.

You may discover scheduling conflicts among courses. Certain courses tend to attract a common group of students. For example, AP English, usually taken in the eleventh grade, and AP U.S. history, also taken in eleventh grade, usually draw from the same pool of students. If the school only offers one section of each course, it should not offer them in the same period because a student may be forced to choose one over the other. A master schedule truly built for students does not include these kinds of course conflicts. Students must have access to every course that they want to take.

Interviews with teachers, counselors, and students will help illuminate how students are actually placed into courses for upcoming school years. Students' experiences with registration can shed light on whether the process of registration helps or hinders their enrollment in the classes that will prepare them for success. A willingness to hear from many parties on what may turn out to be an antiquated, inflexible master schedule will be crucial to your reform effort.

FOCUS GROUPS

Focus groups add a qualitative aspect to the data analyses activities of the audit. They help ascertain where major stakeholder groups line up on the issue of increased rigor in high schools.

Getting Everyone on Board

The next step in the educational opportunity audit is to check in with the students, parents, teachers, counselors, and other members of the community to learn about their experiences and expectations.

Everyone invested in the future of the district's students must be on board for your reforms to succeed. This process begins with holding focus groups so that you can examine the attitudes and beliefs of your district's key stakeholders. A *series* of focus groups is necessary to define the challenges and opportunities to be addressed. Focus groups are the first step in a larger public-engagement effort designed to build a consensus.

Setting up Focus Groups

The focus groups need to include the voices of all important stakeholder groups. The selection process should follow the parameters described here:

- *Students.* Select students representative of the demographics of the entire student body from all grade levels and from all academic pathways—gifted and talented education (GATE), ELL, special education, regular education, CTE, and college prep.
- *Teachers.* Select representatives from each department; ensure that all core disciplines are represented; include both new and experienced instructors.
- *Counselors.* Bring the entire counseling department and the registrar.
- *Parents and community members.* Select parents representative of the demographics of the entire student body as well as parents of children in special education and ELL.
- Select *other community stakeholders,* such as higher education partners and business leaders.

The number of times each focus group meets will depend on the size of your district and the number of high schools involved. If there are a small number of high schools, then each focus group will be held at each of the high schools. For example, if there are three high schools in the district, four focus groups will meet at each high school (one group for students, teachers, counselors, and parents and community members) for a total of twelve focus groups overall. Each session should have ten to fifteen participants. See Appendix 1 for focus group protocols.

COMMUNITY CONVERSATION

A community conversation is like a town-hall meeting in politics—a chance to bring together a large group at a public forum to talk about requiring more rigorous standards in the district's high schools. Bringing everyone together into one room is a key component of public engagement work.

From the district's point of view, this is a chance to emphasize the vision of college- and career-ready education for all students—including closing the achievement gap and improving outcomes for all students. For those who have a stake in this process, this is a chance for their voices to be heard.

You'll need to plan on two community conversations. The first one builds off the focus groups and explores the readiness of stakeholders to support high school reform. This initial conversation is conducted during the educational opportunity audit phase.

The second conversation will be held during the blueprint phase. This will continue to build the support of all stakeholders in the district's reform. See Appendix 2 for the community conversation protocol.

SURVEYING DEPARTMENT HEADS

Getting the input of department heads at this point in the audit is crucial. By conducting surveys, your data team will examine the current status of various departments that will be significantly affected by a shift in curriculum.

The surveys should cover the following areas:

- Curriculum and instruction (benchmarks, textbooks, lesson plans, and so on) for all populations, including special needs, English language learners, and students in CTE programs
- Student support and safety nets
- Teacher capacity and professional development
- Facilities
- Budget

Your data team will collect these surveys from the appropriate department head for each area. After responses are collected, there may be a need to follow up with in-person interviews to clarify and expand on the responses. See Appendix 3 for survey protocols.

EDUCATIONAL OPPORTUNITY AUDIT FINDINGS

Getting this far in the educational opportunity audit helps you to see where you are starting from:

- *The transcript study* has given you a comprehensive picture of what your students' current journey through high school looks like.

- *The master schedule analysis* has given you an understanding of the structure of your high schools.

- *Focus groups* and large-scale *community conversation* have given you stakeholder input and buy-in.

- A *survey of programs and services* provided by the district has solidified your sense of infrastructure.

Findings from all of these audit components should be compiled by your leadership group and data team and submitted to the superintendent and board of education. This report serves as the baseline for development of the blueprint for implementation: an action plan that takes you from where you are now to where you want to be.

READER REFLECTION

1. How important is the educational opportunity audit for creating the impetus for reform?

2. Which parts of the audit are most compelling? Why?

3. Are there things you would add to make the audit comprehensive? Describe.

CHAPTER SIX

The Blueprint

"The requirements are hard, but they are great. They help you, they build you, and they make you who you are. It felt like it was steps. It all added up."

—Latina graduate, 2004

HERE'S WHERE THE REAL CHANGE BEGINS

Now that your district has completed the educational opportunity audit, you should have a strong sense of what is necessary for action. This brings you to the next phase in the reform process—the blueprint.

The blueprint is a plan that describes in detail the steps necessary to transform your district. The blueprint is meant to be a comprehensive, step-by-step course of action based on a deep understanding of the evidence collected and documented in the educational opportunity audit.

This chapter will take you through a recommended committee structure and protocols that will help you get the blueprint written. Getting key stakeholders in your district involved in the steering committee and the various working committees is absolutely crucial because the blueprint is *not* some perfunctory report meant to sit on a shelf after it has been rubber-stamped and filed.

The blueprint maps out the work necessary to bridge the gap between where your district is now and where it needs to be in order to implement a curriculum to ensure that all students are college and career ready.

SETTING UP COMMITTEES TO GET THE WORK DONE

The development of the blueprint should involve internal and external stakeholders. Internal expertise is needed to ensure the action plans are comprehensive and realistic, address all of the issues uncovered in the audit, and have support of those who will be responsible for implementation. External expertise is needed to validate the viability and coherence of the action plans from an outside perspective and to ensure that the broader community has an investment in their successful implementation.

The Steering Committee

The steering committee, appointed by the superintendent, oversees the development of the blueprint. This committee is not merely an oversight body but also a liaison to the larger community, with the responsibility to communicate with constituents about proposed reforms. Committee members must be lead advocates for your reform agenda, and they must take charge of bringing community concerns back to the district.

Suggested Steering Committee Participants

- Superintendent
- Assistant superintendent
- Elementary principal
- Middle school principal (or assistant principal)
- High school principal (or assistant principal)
- Alternative high school principal (or assistant principal)
- Elementary teacher
- Middle school teacher
- High school teacher
- Student
- Higher education—two-year college representative
- Higher education—state university representative
- County office of education
- School board member
- Parents
- Business community member
- Chamber of commerce member
- Trades and apprenticeship representative
- Adult school representative
- Union representative
- Community-based organization representative

If the district identifies other stakeholders who should be part of this committee, please invite them to participate. Adjust this roster to your district's needs and profile.

Working Committees

Working with school districts in California and elsewhere, I have seen the audit process spark deep and meaningful conversations concerning the changes that are necessary in these areas that affect teaching and learning:

- Curriculum and instruction
- Student support and safety net interventions
- Special needs, alternative, English language learner students
- Teacher capacity and professional development

Your working committees will consist of district-level staff, school administrators, teachers, counselors, and students appointed by your superintendent. They will report their findings and recommendations to the steering committee and ultimately to the superintendent and board of education.

If some people on your working committees were not part of the data team that put together the educational opportunity audit, you may have to reframe the conversation for them before they can help write your district's blueprint. Begin  with the guiding questions that can be found on our Web site (www .edtrustwest.org) to help these committee members in their early thinking about how to map out an action plan for college and career readiness.

In general, each working committee will do the following:

- Review audit findings and recommendations.
- Conduct research on best practices.
- Draft action plans for review by the steering committee and other working committees and modify those plans based on this input.
- Prepare final blueprint documents for approval by the superintendent and steering committee and for adoption by the board of education. (After adoption, the steering committee will continue to monitor implementation of the blueprint and report on progress periodically.)

Committee 1: Curriculum and Instruction.

- Articulate the program of instruction and recommended course sequences to prepare all students for college and career readiness. Career-technical pathways may be embedded in the recommended rigorous course sequences so that work-ready skills are addressed as well as core academic requirements.

- Look at links among elementary, middle, and high school processes, including curriculum mapping.

- Engage teachers in examining the core curriculum in elementary and middle school that will prepare students for rigorous high school coursework.

- Look at best practices that engage teachers in examining student work to ensure that assignments and assessments meet rigorous standards at all grade levels. What does "rigorous" work look like? This section of the blueprint should establish rubrics that calibrate the grading practices of teachers with respect to student assignments. You should set up cross-grade and cross-teacher teams examining student work to develop consensus on this.

- Examine benchmark-testing practices and establish recommendations of common assessments that will drive instructional improvements at the elementary, middle, and high school levels.

- Define a process to establish standards for instructional programs, materials, and resources to be consistently available in all elementary, middle, and high schools.

Committee 2: Support and Safety Net Interventions for Regular, Special Needs, Alternative, and ELL Students

- Develop a comprehensive system of student interventions and safety nets so that students with varying achievement levels on entering high school can be successful in a rigorous common core high school curriculum.

- Determine if existing programs and practices are relevant to improvements in student performance by comparing them to other practices and programs in high-performing districts across the country.

- Examine master schedules for district high schools in order to incorporate into the blueprint opportunities for student support classes within the school day, for example, shadow classes.

- Identify class and resource needs outside the regular day, such as before or after school and on weekends.

- Look at summer school to determine whether it is currently functioning as an acceleration strategy for students who struggle with rigorous coursework.

- Explore a variety of research-based strategies for accelerating student learning.

- Develop an outreach plan to engage external partners—community colleges, higher education, businesses—in providing safety net and student support services, such as tutoring, mentoring, and intervention programs.

- Address the requirements of special needs students, English language learners, and alternative education students, whose circumstances require curricular modifications and, in extreme cases, individual graduation plans.

- Examine model programs, best practices, and effective strategies for gaining access to rigorous curriculum for special needs students and English language learners.

Committee 3: Teacher Capacity and Professional Development

- Examine the current capacity of high school teachers to implement rigorous course content with a variety of learners in terms of content knowledge and map out professional development strategies to help fill capacity gaps.

- Create a comprehensive professional development plan addressing student needs uncovered in the audit.

- Incorporate districtwide training needs in areas such as differentiation of instruction, ELL strategies, and expanding teacher understanding of how to use data for improving instruction.

- Address teacher expectations and beliefs.

WORK TO BE DONE BY DISTRICT DEPARTMENTS

Some of the blueprint development work does not need to be filtered through a committee structure and should be done by district departments. These departments are a crucial part of the blueprint process and will, similar to working committees, report directly to the steering committee.

Teacher Recruitment and Staffing in Shortage Areas

- Develop a realistic recruiting plan to meet shortages in staffing based on the gap between the district's current teacher resources and the resources required for the full implementation of the rigorous common core curriculum for all high school students, as revealed by the educational opportunity audit.

- Incorporate an ongoing process to examine attrition factors, pipeline issues with local teacher-training institutions, and compile results of recruitment efforts.

- Address the strategic replacement of teachers for vacancies created by normal attrition and create pathways for current teachers who may be close to certification in a shortage area.

- Engage local teacher-training institutions to help current teachers gain credentials in areas of need.

Funding Requirements to Implement the Reform

- Identify funding sources within the district budget that need to be redirected to the blueprint goals.

- Address all categorical funds, state and federal grants, and any other discretionary revenues currently available and identified through the educational opportunity audit.

- Develop outreach strategies in order to secure external funding, including federal and state grant opportunities, business partnerships, and foundation support.

Taking Inventory of Bricks and Mortar

- Analyze needs for upgrades and addition of science lab facilities to implement the lab science requirements for the new graduation standards.

- Formulate a strategy for necessary improvements, including intermediary solutions for inadequacies in lab facilities. This might include a facility bond, joint-use facility agreements with community colleges, distance learning opportunities, and so on.

■ Define and address other facility needs beyond science labs to accommodate programs such as career-technical education.

Public Engagement and Outreach

■ Create communications planning with clear messaging.

■ Develop public data reports to track district progress.

■ Provide leadership training for principals and district leaders.

■ Develop ongoing community engagement initiatives.

DEVELOPING ACTION PLANS

You now need to move your working committees from analysis to implementation. Each committee should apply the following step-by-step guide to their area of specialty. The resulting action plans will make up the heart of the blueprint. To be most effective, action plans should share a common format, such as the template you will find on the Web site (www.edtrustwest.org).

Step 1: Educational Opportunity Audit Review

■ Review the educational opportunity audit findings in detail.

■ Agree, as a committee, on the major themes that run through the educational opportunity audit.

■ Use those themes to identify critical focus areas that need detailed action plans.

Step 2: Resource Material Review

■ Gather research on best practices, both within the district and from state and national publications.

Step 3: Preliminary Action Plan Development

- Develop a preliminary draft of the action plan that includes the following:
  - Focus area
  - Action steps
  - Timelines
  - Roles and responsibilities
  - Outcome measures

Step 4: Preliminary Draft-Review Process

- Share preliminary drafts of action plans with the superintendent, steering committee, and other working committees.
- Collect input to clarify, revise gaps, eliminate overlap, and align among working committees.

Step 5: Modifications to the Drafts

- Work toward and agree on draft modifications during a facilitated session that involves leaders from each working committee.

Step 6: Final Draft Development

- Incorporate modifications into detailed action plans.
- Forward completed blueprint section (one from each working committee) to the superintendent and steering committee for approval.

Step 7: Approval of the Blueprint

- Take the blueprint to the board of education for approval.
- Begin implementation according to timelines.

Step 8: Ongoing Monitoring of Blueprint Implementation

- Conduct a quarterly review of milestones and outcome measures.
- Issue progress reports to the board of education.

The Timeline

The timeline for the entire audit and blueprint process will vary from district to district depending on size and resources that can be devoted to the completion of the work. A sample timeline is presented in Table 6.1.

TABLE 6.1: Sample Timeline

WHAT	WHEN	WHO
First meetings	End of previous school year	Superintendent leadership group
Gathering artifacts	Summer	Research team
Gathering artifacts	Summer	Leadership group
Principal interviews	Summer	Leadership group
Classroom visits	October–November	Leadership group
Focus groups	October–November	Data team
Surveys to department heads	November	Data team
Transcript study 1	December–January	Data team
Survey follow-up interviews	January–February	Data team
Community conversation 1	December–January	Superintendent
Transcript study 2 (if needed)	February	Data team
First audit report	April–May	Steering committee to the school board
Steering committee meeting 1	May	Steering committee

(*continued*)

TABLE 6.1 (*continued*)

WHAT	WHEN	WHO
Blueprint working group session 1	September	Blueprint working groups
Steering committee meeting 2	September	Steering committee
Blueprint working groups session 2	October	Blueprint working groups
Steering committee meeting 3	October	Steering committee
Blueprint working groups session 3	November–December	Blueprint working groups
Steering committee meeting 4	November–December	Steering committee
Final blueprint submitted to school board	December	Superintendent

◼ READER REFLECTION

1. How important do you feel stakeholder involvement is during the development of the blueprint?

2. Does the process for writing the blueprint as described in this book make sense? Is there anything missing?

3. How should the finished blueprint be communicated to various stakeholders? Who are the most important ones to inform?

CHAPTER SEVEN

A Look at "District X"

"It's not like we're running in test mode here. It's the kids' lives."

—Oakland parent, 2009

THIS IS WHAT IT LOOKS LIKE

Since 2004, several public school districts in California have made the commitment to a college- and career-readiness high school curriculum. Through my work with The ETW, I have been privileged to watch these districts in action, doing the hard work of reform. Each of them was working off the San Jose model: undertaking a districtwide educational opportunity audit, then developing a blueprint. For this chapter, I've taken the findings and recommendations of various districts I've worked with and brought them together into a composite, "District X," to illustrate the various tools outlined in the previous chapters. Though the problems faced by every district are unique, the findings and recommendations I've drawn from here are emblematic of the challenges faced by many.

DISTRICT X: TRANSCRIPT STUDY

After looking at a representative sample of transcripts, District X's data team noted these findings and made the following recommendations.

Finding 1: Math

- The UC/CSU A–G course sequence requires three years of college-preparatory mathematics through a minimum of algebra II. District X requires only algebra I for graduation. This gap between district expectations and college requirements accounts for the largest chokepoint for District X's students.

Student transcripts did not show a logical true sequence of math courses. The data team identified regressive math sequences (in which students take a course that is at a lower level than the one they took previously). In Figure 7.1, the student could have enrolled in algebra II in the senior year, yet took a lower level math course. This was not uncommon on senior transcripts.

Recommendation 1

District X must eliminate regressive math course sequences. Students should be placed into a higher level math course in each successive year. If a student

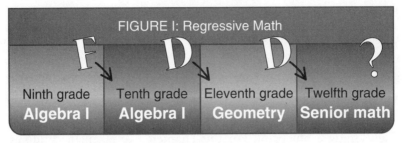

FIGURE 7.1 Regressive Math

has completed geometry at the end of the junior year, the student should be placed into algebra II in the senior year. He or she should not be enrolled into senior math just to earn the math credits for graduation.

Finding 2: World Language

- The A–G course sequence requires two years of the same world language, while District X requires one year of either a world language or an arts class for graduation. Some students took no world language courses; other students took only a single year. Students took enough for graduation but not for college eligibility.

- Some students did take two years of a world language but did not enroll until junior year. If the student struggled in the course, there was limited time to make up the course prior to graduation.

- English language learners are not provided with additional avenues to earn credit for a world language, especially for ones in which they are fluent or proficient.

Recommendation 2

- The district should require two years of a world language.

- The district must provide ELL with additional opportunities to meet this requirement by taking tests such as AP or SAT Subject Tests. This will allow ELL students room in their schedules to take classes that provide support in English or other subjects in which they struggle.

TABLE 7.1: Examples of Senior Schedules Lacking in Rigor

STUDENT A	STUDENT B	STUDENT C
• Library practice	• Senior math	• Late arrival
• Office practice	• Teacher's assistant	• Marching band
• American government	• Short story	• Senior math
• Marching band	• Office practice	• Office practice
• Teacher's assistant	• Early departure	• Latin American literature
• Art fundamentals		• Food service
		• Early departure

Finding 3: Senior Year

Too many seniors were enrolled in courses that lacked any rigor (see Table 7.1).

Recommendation 3

■ Research consistently demonstrates a high correlation between a rigorous senior year and success in college. The rigor of the senior year for students in District X must be increased. Students should take a minimum of four academic core courses (English, math, social studies, science, or world language) and one or two CTE or elective courses.

Finding 4: Interventions

■ The educational opportunity audit found no tools to measure intervention programs, which greatly inhibited the district's ability to identify and replicate effective intervention.

■ If interventions were provided, they were not noted on transcripts.

■ The only interventions identified on transcripts were when students took intervention classes. For some students, the intervention class supplanted rather than supplemented the regular course. Students need additional time in the subject in which they struggle, not simply a replacement class that denies them access to otherwise rigorous coursework.

■ Intervention courses remain reactive rather than proactive solutions; the red flag for most interventions was when a student failed the high-stakes exit exam.

■ Interventions were not timely and thus not effective.

Recommendation 4

- A closer examination of intervention programs must occur to determine their effectiveness.

- The process of placing students into interventions is not clear, and many students who need additional support have no access to it.

- Intervention programs have to be available in a timely manner and allow students to move in and out of the intervention as needed.

- Schools should identify students who need additional math support prior to the first time the CAHSEE (California High School Exit Exam) is taken, in tenth grade, rather than waiting until students' senior year.

DISTRICT X: MASTER SCHEDULE

After looking at District X's master schedule, master calendar, bell schedule, and other organizational structures, the data team noted these findings and made the following recommendations.

Finding 1: Bell Schedules

- Each high school in District X uses a different bell schedule or has a different number of class periods. Some schools offer six periods, others seven, and some eight. Yet schools offering more than six periods use their additional time inefficiently. Some schools offer few classes during the zero or final periods.

Recommendation 1

- Examining ways to better use these periods (such as increasing the number of classes offered at these times) can provide students with opportunities to take additional classes, either for advancement or remediation.

Finding 2: Courses That Meet California's A–G Requirements

- District X's high schools have a high percentage of courses that meet the A–G requirements in science, social science, and world languages. In other areas—including English, math, and electives—District X does not have as high an approval rating. Some district high schools offer students more opportunities than others.

Recommendation 2

- The more classes approved for the A–G sequence that District X high schools can offer, the more opportunities students will have to take the courses necessary to graduate prepared for college and careers. All high schools in the district must offer students the chance to enroll in the courses that are needed for college and meaningful careers.

Finding 3: Schedule Conflicts

- District X's high school master schedules create scheduling conflicts that inhibit students' opportunities to take college-prep courses. For example, at one high school, AP English literature and AP Spanish language are offered only once and during the same period. Students therefore cannot take both courses.

Recommendation 3

- The master schedule must be constructed so that students can take the courses they choose with as few schedule-limiting conflicts as possible.

DISTRICT X: FOCUS GROUPS AND COMMUNITY CONVERSATION

What comes out of focus groups and the initial community conversation will be examined by your data team, which will report findings and make recommendations. District X's conducted focus groups and noted the following.

Finding 1: Student Focus Group

- All students in the focus groups said they were planning to attend college, but they felt that better information should have been given to them and their parents about what it takes to get into college.

- Students need access to the courses that are necessary to be successful in college, and these courses are often not made available to them.
- Students say they could do much more in high school if more were expected of them.

Finding 2: Teacher Focus Group

- Teachers expressed concern that if all students were to take more rigorous or advanced courses, many teachers would feel pressure to water down the curriculum.
- Teachers feel that students need to come to high school better prepared. Too many students enter ninth grade with low-level skills.

Finding 3: Counselor Focus Group

- Counselors see a need for consistency in policies that govern student advancement through high school. They cite the need for consistent rules about how students qualify for AP classes.
- Counselors expressed concern about the lack of consistency in transcripts, such as how courses and other information are noted.

Finding 4: Parent Focus Group

- Parents agreed with students, teachers, and counselors that all students should take the A–G course sequence for graduation but expressed concerns about access to college-preparatory courses. Specifically, they felt that District X's Latino students are neglected.
- Parents echoed student concerns that they need more information about what is necessary for college eligibility and career preparation.

RECOMMENDATIONS BASED ON ALL FINDINGS

- A–G courses should be the basis of graduation requirements for all students. A–G courses should be rigorous and demanding. At the same time, appropriate and essential assistance should be given to teachers and students to meet new challenges.

TABLE 7.2: District X: The Blueprint

Curriculum and Instruction

FOCUS AREA I: HIGH SCHOOL CREDIT REQUIREMENTS

ACTION STEPS	OUTCOMES	WHO	WHEN	RESOURCE NEEDS	CHALLENGES
Beginning with the graduating class of 2016, require all students to complete a college-prep core curriculum to graduate.	Students will be prepared for college.	Superintendent School board	June 2011	Intervention classes Teacher support	Science lab facilities World language teachers

FOCUS AREA 2: CURRICULUM AND ALIGNMENT

ACTION STEPS	OUTCOMES	WHO	WHEN	RESOURCE NEEDS	CHALLENGES
Eliminate regressive math sequences and require students to take three or more years of progressively more rigorous math.	By their senior year, all students will be enrolled in algebra II or higher.	District math specialists High school math department heads	September 2012	Math support classes Teacher professional development Additional teachers	Content knowledge of math teachers to teach higher levels Low expectations for student success
Add enough world language sections to give students access.	Students will all have at least two years of a sequential world language by graduation.	District world language specialists Master scheduler	September 2012– September 2015	World language teacher recruitment	Shortage across the state
Require students to take a full schedule in their senior year.	Students will be better prepared to transition to college and career.	Site administrator Counselors	September 2015	More sections available for seniors	Pushback from students and parents

(Continued)

TABLE 7.2: *(continued)*

Professional Development for Teachers

FOCUS AREA I: SITE-BASED SUPPORT FOR TEACHERS

ACTION STEPS	OUTCOMES	WHO	WHEN	RESOURCE NEEDS	CHALLENGES
Increase collaboration time.	Teachers will be part of professional learning communities focused on improved student learning.	District leaders Site administrator Master schedulers	2012	Master schedule expertise to create common planning time	Difficult to make work
Provide good data for instructional decision making.	Decisions about students will be aligned to performance.	District leaders Site leaders	2012	Data analysis capabilities to be fully developed	Making reports useful to teachers

FOCUS AREA 2: HIGH-QUALITY PROFESSIONAL DEVELOPMENT

ACTION STEPS	OUTCOMES	WHO	WHEN	RESOURCE NEEDS	CHALLENGES
Place emphasis on site-based professional development driven by teacher needs.	Teachers will have buy-in.	Site leaders Department heads Teachers	2012	Time to plan quality professional development	Freeing up staff to participate fully
Provide coaching and mentoring.	Teachers will grow in their expertise by learning from peers.	District leaders Site leaders Department heads	2012	Funds to free up teachers to coach and mentor	Very tight budgets

TABLE 7.2: *(continued)*

Student Support and Safety Net Interventions for Regular, Special Needs, Alternative, and ELL Students

FOCUS AREA I: EXTRA SUPPORTS FOR STUDENTS WHO STRUGGLE IN RIGOROUS COURSEWORK

ACTION STEPS	OUTCOMES	WHO	WHEN	RESOURCE NEEDS	CHALLENGES
Extend day to seven periods for students who need extra support in rigorous coursework.	Struggling students will have more time to master content on a just-in-time basis.	Counselors	2012	Financial support to add needed classes	Finding ways to mitigate costs, such as overlapping teacher schedules
Ensure support systems are organized and systematic so they go into effect for every struggling student at the appropriate time.	Students who start to struggle will get back on track.	Teachers Counselors Site administrators	2012	Procedures that automatically trigger the need for intervention	Making sure students don't fall through the cracks

- Teachers need preparation and professional development time to achieve a variety of critical outcomes: articulation of problems and solutions, collaboration, data analysis, and examination of student work.

- Because more students will graduate with increased options (college and career choices), more time with counselors should be guaranteed. Moreover, counselors should be involved in the development of the master calendar so that students will be provided with efficient use of school time (during the school year and summer) for remediation and for advancement at a faster pace.

- In addition to better information about A–G courses, students and parents need information about college application procedures, including selecting a college, filling out forms (applications and essays), securing letters of recommendation, taking appropriate admissions examinations, and obtaining financial aid and scholarships.

The recommendations that came out of District X's audit were used by working committees to develop the blueprint. The template for the blueprint is available on the Web site (www.edtrust.org/west).

Excerpts shown here are sections of the blueprint for curriculum and instruction, student support and safety net interventions, and professional development (see Table 7.2).

READER REFLECTION

1. How did this example of the audit and blueprint process in action strike you? Was anything surprising?

2. Does the work clearly culminate in a roadmap for reform?

3. Having seen how the tools are applied, could you do this work in your district?

CHAPTER EIGHT

College and Career Readiness in Our Nation's Schools

HOW IS COLLEGE AND CAREER READINESS PLAYING OUT IN OTHER DISTRICTS?

Can San Jose's success be duplicated elsewhere? It's a question worth considering. You might reasonably wonder whether our achievement was an anomaly, the result of a set of variables and unique circumstances conducive to positive change. The fact that San Jose Unified was under a federal court order to desegregate our schools gave us a foundation from which to jump-start our equity agenda (see Chapter Two). The unusually strong partnership that developed between the administration and the teachers' union might not be easily replicated elsewhere (see "From Combat to Collaboration" in Chapter Two). The location of the district in the heart of the Silicon Valley made it possible for us to build partnerships with major businesses and to recruit science and math talent to bridge teacher shortage gaps after the reform was implemented (see Chapter Four). Additionally, the longevity of superintendent leadership we enjoyed is uncommon in urban districts, and reform is inarguably more challenging when there are frequent changes in leadership.

Every district has a unique profile. The variables we faced in San Jose didn't necessarily have to add up to success; what we did within our particular context made the difference. In your district, the circumstances at hand are the ones you have to work with, and any situation can be turned to an advantage if the right strategy and the will to implement it are in place.

Since my retirement as San Jose Unified's superintendent, I've worked with The ETW in nine California districts and two out-of-state pilot high schools within a district to help implement college- and career-ready graduation requirements for all students. Each locale has presented its own set of challenges and opportunities. I'll highlight them here to show how our success with closing achievement gaps in San Jose has taken hold and moved forward in a wide array of communities.

Two Medium-Sized, Demographically Diverse Districts

Two of the districts we worked with shared a similar profile: medium sized and bifurcated by income and ethnicity. Neighborhoods close in proximity were a million miles apart in terms of aspirations. Working-class Latino families, often facing language barriers, were largely disenfranchised and in general feeling unwelcome in their districts. No community organizations represented their interests or fought for equality of opportunity for their children; students and parents alike were unaware that college could be a possibility. On the other side of the divide, affluent parents, most of them white and generally well educated, were reluctant to change anything about the education their children were getting.

In the first of these districts, interest in college- and career-ready graduation requirements began when two high school principals attended an ETW forum on college and career readiness for all and returned to the district excited to share the possibilities of this reform with their colleagues. These principals initially led the charge, and their superintendent took up the gauntlet, bringing in stakeholders, including the president of the teachers' union. The early discussions led to a formal engagement with The ETW.

As the audit work was unfolding, an unusually high level of opposition emerged from one well-respected official in the county. This single outspoken individual, who saw the introduction of college-prep curricula for all as ridiculous, attempted to derail the process from the get-go.

What happened next was instructive. The superintendent put the individual in question on the steering committee for the blueprint. Rather than leaving her on the outside, he brought this respected leader into the process, critical though she was. Other stakeholders listened to her strong opinions, but, in the end, when it was time to vote on the blueprint and set the plan for college and career readiness in place, everyone else on the committee voted thumbs up. The lesson here is clear: even when powerful people oppose this kind of reform, you are wise to bring them to the table. You may not change their minds but you'll give them a voice; the process can accommodate this. Additionally, the inclusion of a dissenting voice has served to make the reforms stronger in this district, ensuring in this case that career-technical training was part of the road to rigor, not a separate track. This district is now implementing its college- and career-readiness program and the community is with them all the way.

In the second of these two districts, the lack of an organized community group representing the interests of poor Latino children was a real barrier to the public engagement process meant to solidify the community behind the reform. This void left the process open to excessive criticism of the district's neglect of the educational needs of Latinos from an organized community group outside the district. During the audit process, a community conversation designed to draw attention to the needs of underserved students was nearly hijacked by an organization from a neighboring town, whose members showed up at the conversation with a press entourage and attempted to create a media event for the purposes of their own agenda. In retrospect, this can be seen as a cautionary tale. If no organized group is already in place in the district to speak for those for whom the reforms are most important, it behooves district leadership to try and fashion one. Finding allies and representation is crucial to building community trust and buy-in from all stakeholders.

In both these districts, leaders stepped forward in a sincere attempt to bring together a more unified community in which all students would receive a quality education. The high school principals became the initial champions of the reform initiative in the first district, and in the second, after that rocky start, an equity-minded associate superintendent became the champion of the reform work that was accomplished there. It may be stating the obvious, but all attempts to implement big reforms need champions!

A High-Poverty Urban District

This urban district, marked by high poverty and a high dropout rate, presented one of our toughest challenges to date. The initial champion of the college- and career-ready agenda was a local community-based organization. This group was instrumental in getting the superintendent, district leaders, and the school board to commit to moving forward with The ETW in pursuit of the goal of rigorous graduation standards.

Among the obstacles in this district was an outdated and poorly designed data system. The administration was in the middle of a technology upgrade as the audit began and, as a result, they were "estimating" college-ready graduates based on inaccurate assumptions that grossly inflated the percentage of students who were really ready for college on graduation. In addition, the transcript review by The ETW was complicated by two different kinds of transcripts, generated by the old and new systems, with different coding and formatting schemes. Understanding students' high school experience took a long time, but when completed the audit revealed accurate information that clearly exposed opportunity gaps. The lack of access to rigorous coursework turned out to be much more severe than what had been previously known and reported by the district, and the audit quickly elevated the importance of addressing the quality of the districts' high schools.

The work in this district was further complicated by the district's decision to initiate another high school reform process at the same time that the college- and career-preparation reform agenda being developed in partnership with The ETW was moving forward. This second initiative was centered on multiple pathways (now called "linked learning" in California), designed to strengthen the career-readiness aspect of high school coursework. Concepts such as applied learning, workplace internships, and integrated curriculum became a major part of the conversation. Although not in conflict with college and career readiness from the academic side—indeed, the model assumes that pathways include college-prep academics—accomplishing both at once is truly complex.

As of this writing, the district is committed to blending career pathways with college-readiness requirements in its overall plan for high school reform and is currently engaged in a deep and thoughtful planning process.

A Large, Highly Diverse Urban District

The work to be done in this large, highly diverse urban district was extremely complicated. There was much to contend with: financial insolvency had put the district into state receivership; many of the district's larger comprehensive high schools had, during the previous decades, been broken into many smaller, theme-focused schools (yet achievement gaps persisted); communities within the district were often at odds with each other; and gang issues presented ongoing problems. Years of attempted reforms had left the community distrustful about initiatives that came and went without major improvements in educational outcomes and opportunities. Introducing a new reform effort that all stakeholders could buy into was an uphill battle. It took strong, well-informed community-based organizations to push the college- and career-ready reform agenda in this environment.

As in the high-poverty urban district mentioned previously, in the midst of The ETW's audit work, an effort was undertaken here to combine college-ready graduation requirements with multiple pathways and linked learning. The new idea began to take shape, and mobilized community groups, already heavily invested in the college-ready aspects of high school reform, became understandably confused about how the multiple pathways and linked learning approach would fit. They feared that linked learning might end up as another way to track students—especially Latino and African American students, who make up significant subgroups of the overall population—into less rigorous preparation.

At one point, a community conversation meant to be an opportunity to talk about high aspirations for students in the district became bogged down as parents and students recounted negative past experiences with the district, leaving little room for a discussion about a better future. These disenfranchised stakeholders believed that previously they had not been granted the ear of the district's leadership to vocalize their concerns, and they responded angrily with painful stories of feeling marginalized and mistreated. The lesson learned here is pretty simple. In communities in which there is a lot of unrest, distress, and confusion about what the district is doing to improve education and meaningfully involve parents in the process, it is imperative that the district sets up opportunities for all voices to be heard, *before* any substantial reform is begun.

Today, this district has moved out of receivership, and a new superintendent, committed to rigorous graduation requirements, is spending a lot of time in the community, listening to what parents and students have to say about improving educational opportunity. The board passed a resolution committing to college and career readiness for all, The ETW audit was completed, the work around linked learning has progressed, and a thoughtful planning process is now underway that includes rigorous academics with career pathways. Though challenges remain, this once-troubled district has certainly come a long way.

A Rural Farming Community

We were invited into this district by a new superintendent with a strong sense of educational equity. She convinced her board to bring in The ETW to help pursue an agenda of college and career readiness for all graduates. We began with a lot of optimism because the commitment was clearly coming from the top, but as it turned out, not everyone in the community was easily swayed. In this district, the majority of students came from families engaged in some form of agribusiness; students traditionally moved along a more or less preordained path from high school to local agricultural jobs. The dominant attitude concerning college readiness was one of skepticism. From parents and teachers, we heard the argument that a high school diploma was all that was necessary to serve their young people well.

What our audit turned up was that a significant portion of their students, including many from the community's large migrant population, were getting a minimal education. The audit exposed huge achievement and opportunity gaps holding students back from a full array of postsecondary college and career opportunities.

We learned, somewhat unexpectedly, through our extensive involvement with stakeholders, that inertia could be quite a force in communities in which strong traditions and values have shaped the educational system. Systemic change cannot happen quickly. At the end of The ETW's audit, this district's leadership decided not to pursue the blueprint process at that time because the community—and many of its own educators—were not ready to embrace full reform. Yet the work here was not without success: the stage had been set for increasing rigor and opportunity. Follow-up contact with district leaders has made clear that there is continued commitment to equity and access and the rigor of coursework in their high schools has improved along with their college-ready graduation rates.

In retrospect, perhaps the greatest value of the work here was that it brought educators and community members together to create a shared understanding that students need to be better prepared for educational and career opportunities beyond high school. From The ETW's perspective, it became clear that rich community traditions could be honored in districts such as this one, even as leaders continue to work on ensuring that students receive a more rigorous education.

Two Affluent Suburban Districts

In two affluent suburban districts, The ETW was brought in by superintendents committed to digging below the generally held perception that the district's relatively high test scores meant that everything was okay and reform was not needed. The issue here was complacency because a majority of parents of students already bound for college held an attitude of, "If it ain't broke, don't fix it." In these districts, strong leadership was crucial to exposing achievement and opportunity gaps and creating a high school experience that worked for all students.

Both of these districts present good examples of what can be accomplished when a very involved superintendent fully commits to college and career readiness for all. In the first case, the superintendent set up meetings with district and school leadership and local businesses—potential partners for reform—before the audit process even began. He spoke personally and passionately at the community conversation about how unacceptable it was that Latino students were falling behind and about his vision that the district would become "world class," maintaining competitiveness in a shifting global economy. He was also a key data and technology advocate, going so far as to help The ETW bring a new level of automation into transcript review, which has proved to be especially useful when auditing larger districts.

Here the audit revealed that two subgroups were underperforming: not only the growing Latino population (which tended to be low income) but also a portion of the more affluent white population for whom the "lure of the beach" outpaced the desire to work hard in school. Transcript data showed that many students in both of these groups were not in fact enrolling in a curriculum that would leave them prepared for college and careers. Similar findings were revealed in the second district, laying waste to the myth that the system needed no fixing.

In the second district, as in the first, a savvy superintendent has been personally involved in every aspect of this reform process. Understanding his community well, he has rolled out the reform agenda without raising concerns, building support at every step of the way through his outspoken commitment and careful planning.

The college- and career-ready efforts in both of these districts has moved to the blueprint implementation stage—a true testament to what can be done when committed leadership stays with the process all the way through.

One of the Largest Districts in the State

This district, one of the largest in California, had changed superintendents many times in recent history; reform agendas came and went with them. The school board passed a resolution that college and career readiness begin with its incoming freshmen, but even after The ETW had begun conducting the audit work, no sense of urgency to get ready for the reforms was apparent. As is often the case in large districts with a lot of leadership changes, we confronted a prevailing culture of "hunker down, do your work and don't worry about this new reform agenda." Thus, it took time to build the commitment for change. It also took time for The ETW to complete a comprehensive audit in a district this large. The data collection and analysis of transcripts involved examining over 6,700 records to determine the journey of students through high schools in the district. The audit with participation of all major stakeholder groups. The hunker-down mentality is no longer pervasive; district, school, and community leaders have become deeply engaged with the shared vision of college- and career-ready graduates.

A Single High School Within a Large Urban District

The effort surrounding college and career preparation in this district was driven by a community determined to hold the leadership accountable to deliver. It began with students, who mobilized to demand that they be given access to the curriculum that would prepare them for college. Hundreds of high school students came to the board of education with a clear message: "Let me choose my future." They told the board that the college-preparatory curriculum was their right. The board responded by adopting a resolution for college and career readiness for all, with a reasonable timetable for implementation.

The ETW was asked to come into a single high school and create a model roadmap for successful implementation of the new policy. The intent was to demonstrate how the audit and blueprint tools could help other schools within the next several years, when the reform would be required districtwide. The work here was marked by a recalcitrant principal who, in the beginning, had his own ideas of where his high school's focus should be. In addition, with the help of The ETW, he also had to figure out how to engage a community divided along racial and socioeconomic lines. Yet over time, with a strong engagement process and the exposure of large opportunity gaps through the audit, educators and parents came together to embrace a college- and career-ready vision for all students.

Two High Schools Outside of California

Our one engagement outside of California took place at two pilot sites in Hawaii. The state comprises one single school district spread out over the Hawaiian Islands. Many of the native students traditionally have not been college bound; school curricular choices have often been limited; and coherent reform efforts have been difficult, in part because of the reality of so many sites spread out over such a large geographic area.

The college- and career-ready reform efforts here were led by principals who took their schools through the audit and blueprint processes in partnership with The ETW. As with the large urban pilot high school in California (mentioned previously), these two schools proved to be a testament to the value of using pilot sites to jumpstart reform across a large and complex system. The feedback from the state is that this kind of deep, engaging work on behalf of students has been one of the best reform processes leaders have seen. As of this writing, serious discussion is now underway to expand the work across the islands into more and more high schools.

YES, YOU CAN

As these profiles show, all kinds of obstacles can be met head on during the road to reform, and many can be overcome, if not always quickly. Not all of these districts have gone the distance to fully implement the college- and career-ready reforms. What they share, however, is an encouraging truth: the push to make diplomas matter for *every* graduating high school senior always has the effect of bringing attention to achievement and opportunity gaps. This work, wherever it is done, clearly exposes institutional barriers to accessing rigor and reduces entrenched community divisions. By focusing on community engagement, shared goals, and solutions, these districts inevitably move toward greater rigor in the curriculum and a new commitment to equality of opportunity for the district's most underserved students. This has been true in communities whose histories vary greatly and whose profiles comprise a wide range of economic, ethnic, and geographic realities. By highlighting them here, I hope I've shown that what we did in San Jose is doable in a variety of settings. Based on experience, I sincerely believe it can be done anywhere.

● READER REFLECTION

1. Which district described in this chapter struck you as facing the biggest challenges? Describe them.

2. Do any of these districts strike you as similar to your own? How might your district respond to similar challenges?

CHAPTER NINE

The Journey Continues

NOW WHAT?

First of all, it bears repeating: college- and career-ready graduation requirements for all students are achievable in urban school districts. After San Jose's first class graduated under the A–G requirements, graduation rates in the district were noted in a national publication to be among the highest in the nation for urban school systems,[1] and they have continued to remain high. Though San Jose Unified is still the only California district to have fully implemented A–G For All, others in California and beyond are in the process of instituting similar efforts (see Chapter Eight).

When I retired in 2004 from my position as superintendent of San Jose Unified, I was given a lot credit for the success that had been achieved under my watch. But as I hope this book makes clear, no single person, even in a leadership role, can drive successful reforms that go as deep as ours did. Everyone with something at stake must be actively committed to working together under the shared belief that all students can succeed at the highest level. But once reform takes hold, where do you go from there? This chapter takes a look at where San Jose is today, more than thirteen years after the board first made the commitment that we'd no longer hand out meaningless diplomas to our students, and more than five years after I handed over the reins to my successor (see "Succession Planning").

Succession Planning

I can't underscore enough how important sustained leadership is in educational reform. All too often, a new superintendent arrives with a mandate from the board to make change, which leads him or her to turn the system on its head in an attempt to create a personal legacy. That kind of disruption can send a signal to the rank-and-file that it is time to hunker down and wait it out, knowing that the reform du jour will soon enough be yesterday's news. Too often, the departure of a superintendent from a

(*continued*)

1. Graduation rates estimated by Christopher B. Swanson, *"Cities in Crisis: A Special Analytic Report on High School Graduation,"* Editorial Projects in Education Research Center, prepared with support from America's Promise Alliance and the Bill & Melinda Gates Foundation, (April 1, 2008).

(continued)

district means that all the work she has done disappears with her. Our reforms were too important not to think about how they were intricately tied to succession planning. That's why I gave my board a lot of notice when I wanted to retire—four years' worth. Four years of notice is unheard of, but we knew we had to create an opportunity for continuity.

The San Jose school board charged me with the responsibility of finding someone who could potentially carry our work forward, someone who shared our beliefs, values, and passion for closing the achievement gap. Even before our official search, I began looking around for such a person. A local colleague, who was a sitting superintendent himself, pointed me to Don Iglesias, who was then an assistant superintendent in nearby Santa Cruz and the president of the Association of California School Administrators. When I interviewed Don, I knew immediately that he had the right stuff. He was passionate about closing achievement gaps; had a solid background as a teacher, principal, and district office leader; and was well respected in his district and throughout the state. I convinced him to join our district as deputy superintendent, even though there was no promise that this position would lead to his becoming superintendent.

We were able to work side-by-side for two years to be sure that we were putting in place everything necessary to continue the success we had begun to see under our new rigorous graduation requirements. During the 2003–04 school year, at the end of which I retired, Don was appointed superintendent-elect. I was overjoyed that he would be my successor. Don has his own unique style of leadership, but he has never missed a beat in carrying the torch for the reforms we had worked so hard on together. He has taken the district to new heights.

My time at San Jose ended after seeing our first three A–G classes graduate with great success. But a lot has happened in the years since. As I was preparing to write this book, I sat down with Don to see how our succession planning had held. I was curious to find out which aspects of the college- and career-readiness reforms he saw as most important, what his successes and challenges had been during his tenure, and which steps still needed to be taken. I've incorporated some of what I learned from him throughout this chapter.

Don started the interview by acknowledging how our over-lapping years of common vision allowed him to carry the work forward in new and exciting ways. The reality of sustained leadership, he noted, was that it brought a tenacious focus to the district's vision, deepening the commitment of the superintendent and the board to efforts already underway.

Interestingly, Don talked about sustained leadership and succession planning for administrators and teachers, too. He spoke of the strong responsibility he felt to groom future principals—leaders whose values and skills made them a good match for a district dead serious about systemic reform. His starting point was making sure that future principals would accept nothing less than excellence from all students. He talked as well about giving these future leaders the opportunity to grow.

During his tenure, Don reached out to Teach for America, bringing in new teachers who already had the right belief system and wanted to work with San Jose's most underserved students. He has continued to place emphasis on supporting new teachers through the beginning teacher support and assessment program, in which mentoring teachers help induct new teachers into the profession. Professional development that is truly teacher driven has been realized under his watch. He believes the vision of leadership at every level is being actualized in San Jose Unified. More than a side effect of curriculum reform, professional development in Don's view is a key component of putting that reform into effect and ensuring student success.

Recently, Don retired after six years as superintendent, which means that between my time and his, the district has seen seventeen years of a common vision and direction—worth noting because in large urban districts, the average tenure is somewhere around three years in length. The luxury of a lengthy transition not only allowed for a smooth and gradual shift in leadership, but it also ensured continuity of vision.

Among the two most important legacies of A–G For All are how changes made at the high school level have transformed the school experience for students all the way down to kindergarten and how the district's teachers have embraced change to the point of becoming truly innovative and savvy about using data. I hope this concluding chapter will provide a sense of the challenges that remain so that other districts can have a sense of what to anticipate in the long run.

From my perspective, it seems that once you raise your standards, you are always in the process of change. You can mark your successes—and you should absolutely celebrate them—but you can't rest with them. In San Jose, the district has been transformed, but the work goes on.

CREATING A COLLEGE-GOING CULTURE

Toward the end of my tenure, I, along with my successor, Don Iglesias, brought a resolution to the school board. We called on the district to identify itself as being in support of a "college-going culture." We wanted this to be stated as an explicit part of our mission so that our students would come to see college as an option—or more accurately, an aspiration—for each and every one of them.

This need arose because despite our successes, not enough of our students were entering college after high school. More were graduating college-*eligible* than ever before but not enough were actually enrolling. We wanted to put college in the sights of our students starting from kindergarten. Now, some people scoffed at ideas such as marking the end of kindergarten with a graduation ceremony, wondering if this wasn't overkill. But we recognized the importance of celebrating milestones from the earliest grades and of signaling even to our youngest students that the completion of one level always points to the next. The message was this: every exit is an entry to somewhere new.

The idea of a college-going culture became an even stronger reality in the years after my retirement. Gone are the days when a "college fair" foisted on high school juniors could be considered enough. With the participation of local universities, many activities now support the idea of college as an inexorable destination:

- Tutors, currently in college, work with young children.
- Successful adult role models from representative communities visit students of all ages in their classrooms.
- Students visit college campuses.
- Parents participate in workshops that teach what they can do to help prepare their children for college.
- Classroom curricula, available to all teachers, include a variety of lessons and activities to build college aspirations in students.

The impact is now being felt—district officials report that college enrollments are indeed rising. Consistent messaging and unrelenting attention to college being a possibility for all is paying off big time in San Jose.

A New Kind of College and Career Center

It's worth mentioning how individual commitment and dedication from teachers and administrators can make a world of difference. In San Jose, one instructor at Willow Glen High School took a huge, empty room and turned it into a lively college and career center—complete with posters, pennants, information, brochures, and ten to fifteen computers to provide students the opportunity to research colleges and careers themselves. Among her efforts were the following:

- Finding grant money to fund the technology—such as upgrading computers and software when necessary—to make the center a success

- Creating a yearly plan for events and activities so that students can attend with parents, with particular attention paid to ELL students who might not readily come into the center on their own

- Hosting a career day with representatives from a wide variety of industries

- Building alliances with teachers to promote college and career readiness in the classroom

- Collaborating with school counselors to plan and implement the guidance curriculum for the year

- Promoting a college-going culture around campus through fliers and posters as well as on school marquees, which also raises community awareness

- Recruiting bilingual assistants and volunteers and providing translators at events to make the center accessible to Latino parents

- Meeting with students every day one-on-one, often before or after the school day, to plan postsecondary transitions to college and careers

A DATA-DRIVEN DISTRICT

Using data to improve instruction in the classroom has always been an important aspect of San Jose Unified. In recent years, the notion of data-driven decision making has come into its own and the district is now nationally recognized for the way it makes use of student data to improve education.

Most districts today consider themselves to be data driven. But from my experience, the depth of analysis and the use of data to drive instructional improvement in the classroom are still cursory in most places. Some of the California districts I've worked with in the past few years have begun combining state test results, benchmark assessments, and disaggregating of data in order to reveal achievement gaps, but even in these locations, creating a real impact on classroom instructional practice—the better to accommodate individual student needs and push toward mastery of standards—remains elusive.

San Jose Unified has a robust data warehouse that holds thirteen years of longitudinal data on students (and counting). The warehouse can be queried to produce reports that are useful to teachers and to site and district administrators. Data can be disaggregated by subgroups and tracked over time. Both standardized and customized reports are generated routinely. Edusoft, a test-generating system, is the backbone of district benchmark assessments in four core subject areas: English language arts, math, science, and social studies. Benchmark assessment data, generated at every six-week grading period, are part of the data warehouse, as are end-of-course assessments in English language arts and math. Currently, other common, core, end-of-course assessments in social studies and science are in development.

Today, teachers meet in teams to help each other analyze student data as part of an ongoing conversation about what works and what needs to change to promote better student success. Understanding how to use data has become an important aspect of teacher collaboration. Transparency of student outcomes has led to some remarkable overall changes in professional practice, as well as a lot of specific examples of how teachers are pushed to understand their own methods. Inquiry data-based decision making has permeated teacher practice at high schools in SJUSD, with data teams in every high school probing and acting on the results of their own queries.

How Teachers Have Been Using Data to Drive Change in Their Classrooms

- An SJUSD social studies teacher was seeing decreasing passing rates in his AP class. He became convinced that a new social studies teacher of an earlier class in the course sequence had poisoned the well, leaving students unprepared for his challenging AP coursework. The data team investigated his hypothesis. It turned out that the current crop of AP students had had several social studies teachers during their first year. Indeed, the data team could find no link among the new teacher, course grades, and AP performance. As a result, the AP teacher had to examine his own practice and work with his social studies colleagues to better prepare students for AP success. His pass rates are now rising.

- The math department of an SJUSD high school wanted to know why girls were taking fewer math courses. The data team decided to explore this phenomenon by identifying equally high-performing boys and girls in freshman math and examining their course-taking decisions in subsequent years. They found that girls were three times less likely to choose advanced math classes. Most stopped taking math when they finished the algebra II requirement. The school moved to create gender-equitable classes and a stronger recruitment process. By 2009, girls made up a majority of precalculus and calculus classes at the school.

WHERE THE WORK IS HEADING

Although there are a lot of positive indicators of continued success in San Jose, I discovered in conversations with teachers that there are still reasons to press forward with changes that improve student performance.

Support systems for struggling students continue to evolve. Shadow classes have been a primary intervention over the years, with math and English language arts support classes built into the schedules of those students who need added support. However, high schools are finding that these are not as effective as originally hoped, so differing approaches are now being tried. Rather than placing a struggling student in a shadow class for a whole year, the district is trying out a six-week module of support, taught as a seventh period and as a Saturday academy. There are signs that this intervention works better, in part because students can move in and out of support classes as needed and no one is locked into a support class for an entire year.

As is true throughout our state and across the country, algebra remains the biggest challenge to students. New programs are being tested in summer school to help struggling students access conceptually challenging algebraic concepts. The backward mapping of algebra-readiness standards is a critical part of district efforts to move toward universal algebra for all eighth-grade students. Partnerships with higher education institutions to train elementary teachers in prealgebra skills are growing, as are implementation of middle school programs that have been developed by Stanford and UCLA. Online professional development in algebra is being provided to eighth-grade teachers as well.

THE GOOD NEWS: UNIVERSAL ACCESS

In the San Jose Unified School District today, nearly all high school students pass the A–G sequence to earn a high school diploma. Only a small number of graduates—including some special needs students, some English language learners, and the small percentage of students in alternative programs—graduate under special provisions of the district's graduation policy. Giving students *access* to the A–G courses is no longer the problem it once had been. More than 90 percent of the students in San Jose's comprehensive high schools take the A–G course sequence. Of note, nearly 70 percent of current ELL students take the full A–G course sequence, and almost 90 percent of students who have moved from the status of ELL to fully English proficient (FEP) take these same classes (see Figure 9.1).

SJUSD students now have near-universal access to college-preparatory curricula. Close to half of the graduates from the district's six comprehensive high schools can apply directly for admission to the California State University systems because they took and passed all of the required A–G classes with a grade of C or better. This represents a major increase from the 30-percent eligibility rates before A–G became the common core curriculum. Grades have actually improved in all core academics, and interestingly the highest increase in grades of C or better occurred in science, in which the majority of students went from taking nonlaboratory life and physical sciences to biology, chemistry, or physics (see Figure 9.2).

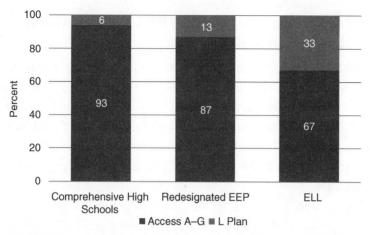

FIGURE 9.1 Percentage of Students in the Class of 2008 in Comprehensive High Schools, Redesignated FEP, and ELL Who Accessed the UC-CSU A–G Courses

Note: In the L plan requirements are modified according to individual student needs.

Source: The Education Trust–West analysis of SJUSD data. *A Case Study: Preparing Students for College and Career,* January 2010. © 2010 The Education Trust–West.

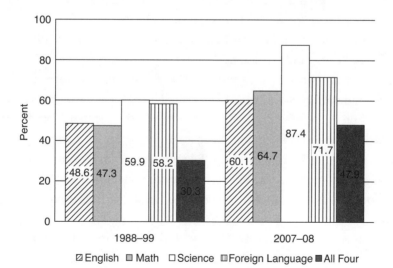

FIGURE 9.2 SJUSD Graduates Satisfying the UC-CSU A–G Subject Requirements from Comprehensive High Schools

Source: The Education Trust–West analysis of SJUSD data. *A Case Study: Preparing Students for College and Career,* January 2010. © 2010 The Education Trust–West.

"D" GRADES REMAIN THE GREATEST BARRIER TO COLLEGE ELIGIBILITY

The greatest barrier to college eligibility in San Jose is below-average grades—D grades in particular—in one or more of the courses that make up the A–G sequence. Without exception, students who fail a required class must repeat the class in order to graduate. They most often do this by attending summer school or retaking the course during the regular school year. SJUSD provides many options so that making up failed courses will not prevent a student from graduating.

But D grades are another story. Although D grades are passing grades for high school credit in SJUSD and count for meeting graduation requirements (as is generally true elsewhere), they are not considered acceptable for admission to the public university system. Both UC and CSU require passing grades of C or better in A–G courses. Unfortunately, students have few avenues to make up Ds because the state does not provide funding for repeating classes that students pass.

It's important to note, however, that even though Ds remain a significant problem, the percentage of Ds and Fs in core courses did *not* increase when the district ratcheted up academic rigor. Receiving a D has nothing to do with *capacity* to learn; *wherever* the bar is set, the same number of Ds occurs statistically. This belies the argument that traditionally underrepresented students cannot handle demanding classes.

In my recent conversations with teachers, they acknowledge that below-average grades often stem from factors such as homework problems, lack of participation in class, and lack of effort to master the content. Very few teachers believe below-average grades have anything to do with ability. In fact, if we look at the distribution of D and F grades earned in core academic classes in San Jose before and after the reform, we see that students got Ds and Fs in low-rigor courses at about the same rate as they did in high-rigor courses (see Figure 9.3).

On a recent visit to San Jose, I met with the new superintendent, who told me about the district's ongoing efforts to address D grades as well as new initiatives that were placing high priority on the middle grades so that they are every bit as rigorous as high school in preparing students for the college-preparatory high school core. The work toward building and sustaining a

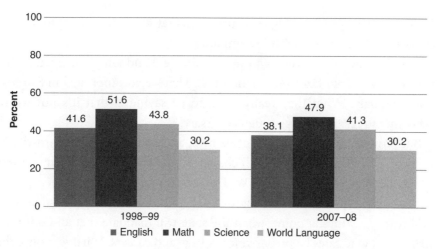

FIGURE 9.3 Percentage of SJUSD Graduates from Comprehensive High Schools with Ds or Fs in Core Courses Has Not Changed Significantly

Note: Core courses generate credit for graduation.

Source: The Education Trust–West analysis of SJUSD data. *A Case Study: Preparing Students for College and Career,* January 2010. © 2010 The Education Trust–West.

college-going culture is far from over. In communities in which low expectations are most devastating to student outcomes, the work is in many ways just beginning.

In writing this book, and taking a new look at the district where it all began, I can see that the journey is ongoing. However, it is far from endangered because it is built on a strong, inarguable vision that is not about the people at the top who are pushing the changes—it's about students who are benefiting from them.

THE PATH IS CLEAR

Perhaps the clearest demonstration of the long-term impact of A–G For All in San Jose came in the conversations I had with teachers and administrators. Again and again, when pressed to answer the question, "Could the district slide back to the old way of thinking about student expectations, with some students being perceived as capable of tackling a rigorous curriculum and others not?" they gave the same answer: a resounding "no!"

As A–G For All has become the norm in San Jose, there has been a philosophical sea change among educators. The focus now is on what students *can* do when challenged with higher expectations rather than on how to accommodate them based on perceived limitations.

I think of this whenever I go out into the field and am confronted by the naysayers who hold fast to the notion that what we accomplished in San Jose is an anomaly. What they really seem to be saying is that it's not worth the bother to try. Inertia is a tough adversary.

But positive change is a force of its own, and with enough forward-thinking people working together, such change can be unstoppable. In my postretirement experience with The ETW, I've seen more and more districts get on board, and I believe we're moving toward critical mass. My hope is that soon we'll reach the tipping point, when the state will mandate that all California high school graduates be prepared for college and careers. What was once the vision of a single district is becoming a movement. The big urban districts have embraced this approach: San Francisco, Oakland, Los Angeles, and San Diego, along with many other smaller districts as well.

When the facts are laid out and the myths are dispelled, the results analyzed, and the stories told, the path is clear. Preparing every high school senior for college and careers is an idea whose time has come. As our nation takes up this gauntlet, America will emerge once again as the best-educated country on the planet.

The world is changing and the way we educate the next generation must change with it. I believe we've found a way to do it.

◼ READER REFLECTION

1. Does the continued work in San Jose seem to include the right things to focus on? Explain.

2. Overall, does this field guide raise your sense of urgency to address the equity agenda?

3. Does this guide give you hope that college and career readiness can be accomplished for all U.S. students?

Appendixes

APPENDIX 1

Focus Group Protocols

To conduct a focus group, you'll need to provide the following:

- Facilitator
- Ten to fifteen participants per focus group
- Private room or area
- Tables and chairs set up in a circle or square

PROTOCOL FOR STUDENT FOCUS GROUP WORK

Each student focus group should involve ten to fifteen students, broadly representing the high school students in the district in terms of the various high school pathways (for example, general education, college prep, vocational, and career-technical).

The facilitator introduces him- or herself and explains the purpose of the focus group and the facilitator's neutral role. The facilitator shares the district's vision of college and work readiness for all students to help frame the conversation. Students are assured of their anonymity but told that the session is being recorded so that all comments are accurately captured.

> *Facilitator:* Hello, my name is _____. We are here to determine current levels of high school preparation and to identify the changes necessary to implement a college- and career-ready curriculum for all students. This group interview will give us insight into your perceptions of your high school experience.
>
> I would like to tape record this group interview to avoid missing anything you say during our conversation. The contents of this interview are for educational purposes only and you will remain anonymous. Are there any questions before we begin?

As a warm-up, the facilitator starts with the following:

1. Going around the table, state your name and tell me one thing about your high school that you particularly like.

2. Okay, now in reverse order tell me one thing about your high school that you particularly dislike.

The facilitator proceeds to explore student attitudes and expectations, indicating that anyone can jump in and offer opinions on the following:

1. How hard is high school? What makes the school hard or easy?

2. Think about the best teacher you've had at this high school. What made this teacher the best? What types of things did he or she do in class that had a positive impact on you? How did the teacher challenge you?

3. Conversely, think about a teacher you have struggled with. Why?

4. Do you get help from your teachers when you don't understand something? What do they do to help you?

5. How do teachers communicate their expectations to you? How much is expected of you in your classes? If teachers expected more of you, would you be able to do it?

6. Which classes do you find most challenging? Why?

7. What are your goals after high school? Are you being prepared to meet your goals by the courses you are taking now? How?

8. What roles do the counselors play in preparing you for life after high school? What types of support do they provide? How often do you see your counselor?

9. Have you had access to the classes that you need to be prepared for life after high school? If not, what has stopped you from taking those classes?

10. What career-technical courses have you taken? How do you know about these courses? How do you get access to the courses?

11. Do you believe you are prepared for college and career?

12. If you could change one thing about your high school, what would it be?

The facilitator asks if the students have other comments about their high school that they would like to share. After final comments, the facilitator thanks the students for their participation.

PROTOCOL FOR TEACHER FOCUS GROUP WORK

Each teacher focus group should involve ten to fifteen teachers, broadly representing the subjects being taught and ensuring that all of the core disciplines are represented.

The facilitator introduces him- or herself and explains the purpose of the focus group and the facilitator's neutral role. The facilitator shares the district's vision of college and work readiness for all students to help frame the conversation. Teachers are assured of their anonymity but told that the session is being recorded so that all comments are accurately captured and that their input will be used to help determine the future direction of the high schools in the district.

> *Facilitator:* Hello, my name is _____. We are here to determine the current levels of high school preparation and to identify the changes necessary to implement a college- and career-ready curriculum for all students. This group interview will give us insight into your perceptions of teacher's roles in providing all students with this opportunity.
>
> I would like to tape record this group interview to avoid missing anything you say during our conversation. The contents of this interview are for educational purposes only and you will remain anonymous. Are there any questions before we begin?

As a warm-up, the facilitator starts with the following:

1. Going around the room, tell us what you teach and how long you have been teaching, and then tell something really great about your high school.

2. Okay, now in reverse order describe something that needs to be improved at your high school.

The facilitator proceeds to explore teacher attitudes and expectations, indicating that anyone can jump in and offer opinions on the following:

1. Do most of your students give you their best effort in class? How do you know that? Do you find that some students try to slide by doing the minimum? What strategies have you found successful in encouraging or motivating those students?

2. Do you feel that most students at your high school are challenged by the courses they take? Could students do more if they were asked to do more?

3. How do students get into AP and honors courses? Is there an open enrollment policy?

4. Are most of your students taking courses to prepare themselves for college?

5. Overall, do you think students are being well prepared for future careers or college? How do you know this?

6. Are you aware of career-technical courses and pathways offered at your school? What are they? How do students enroll in them? Is there any

collaboration between academic and career-technical teachers on your campus?

7. What types of support are available to students who are struggling? Do you feel that students get enough support outside of what you are able to give them so that they can be successful if they apply themselves, for example, for things such as tutoring, extra classes, counseling, and so on?

8. How do you communicate your expectations to students? Do you hold all students to the same performance expectations?

9. Do you believe that all students at this high school should graduate with opportunities to go on to postsecondary education and training? Why or why not?

10. What supports do you need in order to teach the diverse student populations represented in your high school to high standards in terms of professional development opportunities, classroom materials, administrative support, and so on?

The facilitator asks if the teachers have other comments about their high school that they would like to share. After final comments, the facilitator thanks the teachers for their participation.

PROTOCOL FOR COUNSELOR FOCUS GROUP WORK

Each counselor focus group should involve all counselors. It is recommended that a counselor focus group for each comprehensive high school be completed in order to probe counselor attitudes about the quality of the counseling program as well as the role the counselor plays in a student's academic choices.

The facilitator introduces him- or herself and explains the purpose of the focus group and the facilitator's neutral role. The facilitator shares the district's vision of college and work readiness for all students to help frame the conversation. Counselors are assured of their anonymity but told that the session is being recorded so that all comments are accurately captured and that their input will be used to help determine the future direction of the high schools in the district.

Facilitator: Hello, my name is _____. We are working to determine current levels of high school preparation and to identify the changes necessary to implement a college- and career-ready curriculum for all students. This group interview will give us insight into your perceptions of counselors' roles in providing all students with this opportunity.

I would like to tape record this group interview to avoid missing anything you say during our conversation. The contents of this interview are for educational purposes only and you will remain anonymous. Are there any questions before we begin?

As a warm-up, the facilitator starts with the following:

1. Going around the room, give your name, tell how long you have been a counselor, and then tell something really great about your high school.

2. Okay, now in reverse order describe something that needs to be improved at your high school.

The facilitator proceeds to explore counselor attitudes and expectations, indicating that anyone can jump in and offer opinions on the following:

1. What do you spend most of your time doing: scheduling, supervision, . . . ? What do you wish you had more time to do?

2. What is the structure of your counseling office? How are students assigned? How do counselors support English learners and special needs students? Is there just one counselor for each of these groups or are these students spread out among all counselors? How effective as a counselor are you in this structure? What changes do you suggest?

3. Describe the role of counselors in helping students in your high schools. Are there policies and procedures in place to assist you with this? If so, what are they?

4. What is the process for placing students on specified tracks (pathways)? Who is involved in this process and who makes the final decision? How do students get into AP and honors courses? Are there prerequisites for these classes? How do you encourage students to take more challenging courses?

5. What policy or procedure does your counseling program have to prevent students from dropping out? Please describe. How effective is it?

6. How do counselors use student achievement data, if at all, to inform your counseling program?

7. What kinds of interactions do you have with teachers concerning student achievement? Are you involved with student placement in courses? What is your role?

8. What is the registration process for student schedules for the upcoming year?

9. What role do counselors have in building the master schedule?

10. Do you prepare four-year plans? Are they useful? How much do you incorporate or use these plans with your students?

11. Do you think all students should have access to college-preparatory courses?

12. Do you think all students should be required to take a college-preparatory course sequence in order to graduate? What could counselors do to assist students who will struggle with these courses?

13. Are your students capable of taking more challenging courses to prepare themselves for any postsecondary option?

14. What career-technical courses are available at your school? Do these courses have a pathway? What are the outcomes for students who take these courses? How do counselors get information about the career-technical courses offered? How is that communicated to students? How do students enroll in these courses?

15. Are you able to talk with your students about college? If so, what kinds of conversations take place? How, as a counselor, are you updated with current information on colleges, financial aid, and so on?

16. What role do parents play? Are you able to discuss college information with parents?

17. What types of things could be done to better support you in your endeavor to help all of your students to graduate ready for college and career?

18. What kinds of professional development do you attend?

19. What are the outcomes expected of counselors at your schools?

The facilitator asks if the counselors have other comments about their high school that they would like to share. After final comments, the facilitator thanks the counselors for their participation.

PROTOCOL FOR PARENT AND COMMUNITY FOCUS GROUP WORK

Each parent and community focus group should involve ten to fifteen members, broadly representing the parents and community stakeholders.

The facilitator introduces him- or herself and explains the purpose of the focus group and the facilitator's neutral role. The facilitator shares the district's vision of college and work readiness for all students to help frame the conversation. Parents and community members are assured of their anonymity but told that the session is being recorded so that all comments are accurately captured and that their input will be used to help determine the future direction of the high schools in the district.

> *Facilitator:* Hello, my name is _____. We are working to determine current levels of high school preparation and to identify the changes necessary to implement a college- and career-ready curriculum for all students. This group interview will give us insight into your perceptions of the district's role in educating the students.
>
> I would like to tape record this group interview to avoid missing anything you say during our conversation. The contents of this interview are for educational purposes only and you will remain anonymous. Are there any questions before we begin?

As a warm-up, the facilitator starts with the following:

1. Going around the room, tell us the best thing about your student's high school or our high schools in general if you are not a parent.

2. In reverse order, what is one thing you would like to see changed?

The facilitator proceeds to explore parent and community attitudes and expectations, indicating that anyone can jump in and offer opinions on the following:

1. Do you believe students in this district are getting the best education possible? Give examples of why you do or do not believe this.

2. Are students motivated to do well in school or do kids seem to slide through school with minimal effort? In what ways can students be motivated?

3. In what ways are you informed about the progress of your own students or students in general? Do you feel like you are well informed about the progress of your own students or students in general? How could this be improved if needed?

4. Would you be in favor of tougher graduation requirements? If so, what else should be required of students in order to graduate from high school? Should they be prepared to go to college?

5. Should all kids take higher-level math in high school? Science? Foreign language?

6. What types of career-technical courses or pathways are available for your students? Do you believe that students who take these courses are being prepared for a career in that particular pathway?

7. Compared to when you were in high school, is it harder? Easier? Why?

8. Should all students be provided the opportunity to go to college when they graduate from high school if this means harder graduation requirements? Given what you know about being successful in the world of work today, should high schools demand more of their students?

9. When students are having a hard time in class, do they get the help they need?

10. What community groups are you involved in? What do they do?

The facilitator asks if parents and community members have other comments about the high schools that they would like to share. After final comments, the facilitator thanks the group for their participation.

Community Conversation Protocol

Plenary session	Sixty minutes
Breakout sessions	Seventy minutes
Closing plenary	Twenty minutes
Total time	Two hours thirty minutes

PLENARY SESSION

The superintendent welcomes the group and outlines the purpose of the meeting. The emphasis of this welcoming statement should be on the district's vision related to closing achievement and opportunity gaps, the goal of improving college- and career-ready outcomes for all students, the importance of engaging the community in the process, and an overview of the successes of students to date as well as the challenges of raising expectations for all students. It should be stated clearly that the district needs to solicit stakeholder input on the district's vision and mission statements in order to guide general district strategic planning during the next two to three years. It should also be clearly stated that the intent is to involve the community in the development of a blueprint for educational excellence, particularly as it relates to expectations for what students should know and be able to do at the culminating point of their K–12 experience. The group should know that their input is important to this end; their ideas will be recorded and used as the district moves into the planning process.

District instructional leaders then should share pertinent data about the school district and the need for high school reform. This presentation should include a review of student performance and school accountability measures as well as an analysis of college readiness among current graduates. Postsecondary data should be presented as well if available. All data and information should be disaggregated for significant subgroups.

BREAKOUT SESSIONS

A facilitator welcomes the group (ten to fifteen members per group) and sets the context and rationale (four minutes).

■   ■   ■

This evening's conversation is designed to give you a chance to discuss learning expectations for our students, especially concerning what all students should know and be able to do when they graduate from high school.

We want to talk about the dreams that we have for our students after graduation and how we can turn our dreams into reality.

Although almost 90 percent of eighth-graders expect to participate in some form of postsecondary education and nearly two-thirds of parents consider college a necessity for their children, only about *X* percent [fill in] of our state's graduates actually do go on to college and *Y* percent [fill in] of them drop out before they receive a certificate or degree.

Research concerning the skills high school graduates need make it clear that college ready and work ready are the same in today's economy and that some level of education after high school will be needed for most good jobs. Universities, community colleges, and technical or apprenticeship programs demand well-educated candidates.

Our district is asking you to help define what "well educated" means for our graduates so that all students are college ready and work ready when they receive their diplomas.

Our discussion tonight will gather your ideas on this topic and give guidance to the district to ensure that our schools are preparing our students so that they can achieve their dreams.

■   ■   ■

The facilitator sets the context for the conversation (six minutes):

- Introduces self
- Explains role: neutral and in charge of process and time
- Determines need for translation
- Assigns a time keeper
- Goes over ground rules:
  - Listen attentively.
  - Keep comments brief and focused to the discussion.
  - Be respectful of others' ideas.

Facilitator leads discussion of three questions (one hour):

1. Expectations for students

Question 1: What changes should the district implement to establish high expectations for all students?

- Have individuals turn to a partner and discuss Question 1 (ten minutes).
- Have each pair share one to two thoughts.
- The facilitator records each pairs' ideas on chart paper. Allow time for discussion of the ideas with the whole group (fifteen minutes).

2. Conversations on needed high school reforms

Question 2: Based on what you've shared, what thoughts do you have about specific things the district should do K–12 to improve the education our students have received by the time they complete our high schools?

The facilitator solicits thoughts from the group and records group comments on chart paper. Group identifies its top two or three reform ideas using sticky dots. Each participant receives three dots and places them next to the top three ideas (ten minutes):

Red dots—teachers

Blue dots—parents

Yellow dots—students

Green dots—community

3. Review of the district's vision and mission

Question 3: Based on the district's vision and mission, what can the community do to support high expectations for all students?

The group brainstorms the community role as a full group with the facilitator recording their ideas on chart paper. The facilitator guides the group to consensus on the three top priorities and notes them on the chart paper (fifteen minutes).

4. The facilitator reviews all of the group work and wraps up the meeting (5 minutes).

CLOSING PLENARY

The superintendent leads a brief discussion of items that came out of the breakout groups. Each group will mention two to three important points. The superintendent thanks them for coming and talks briefly about how their input will be used and what the next steps are.

Participants should be given an opportunity to look at the work of the other groups and encouraged to leave sticky note comments next to areas of particular interest or sticky notes with their names, phone numbers, and e-mails next to areas in which they would be willing to help with future planning work.

Participants should be asked to complete an evaluation of the community conversation.

APPENDIX 3

Survey Protocols

The following survey instruments are given to appropriate district department heads to collect information relevant to the audit. Department heads fill out the surveys and return them to the leadership group.

BUDGET SURVEY

Please answer the following questions about how financial resources flow to the district and schools based on instructional priorities.

1. What are the restricted and unrestricted sources of state and federal funding the district currently receives? How much discretion does the district provide in allocating its funding to schools? Do schools have flexibility in setting budget priorities?

   _____

   _____

   _____

2. What other external funding, such as competitive grants, does the district or schools receive?

   _____

   _____

   _____

3. Does the budget process follow instructional priorities? Describe the process.

   _____

   _____

   _____

4. What special programs are in place to help struggling students and how are these programs funded (competitive grants, state and federal categorical funds, general funds, foundations, other sources)?

   _____

   _____

   _____

5. How is summer school funded? Can summer school funds be used for advancement, remediation, or both?

   _____

   _____

   _____

6. Are there other avenues for revenue the district should pursue to increase monies to use for college and career readiness?

   _____

   _____

   _____

CURRICULUM AND INSTRUCTION SURVEY

Please answer the following questions about district instructional priorities and accountability at the site and classroom levels.

1. What are the districtwide curriculum and instruction priorities?

    _____
    _____
    _____
    _____
    _____

2. What progress has been made in terms of curriculum calibration? Do teachers meet to discuss what performance levels provide proficiency in terms of state performance standards?

    _____
    _____
    _____
    _____
    _____

3. What are the K–12 articulation initiatives? What progress has been made in terms of curriculum mapping?

    _____
    _____
    _____
    _____
    _____

4. Does the district or school use the any reading and writing curriculum in the twelfth grade? How have the teachers been trained in the use of this curriculum? How do you know if it is successful?

    _____
    _____
    _____
    _____
    _____

5. What benchmark testing is used in the district? How are the tests developed, used, and stored? What database management system is used in the district? How do teachers access these data?

    _____
    _____

_____

_____

6. Are common textbooks used by high schools in this district for the core subject areas? What is the adoption process? Are there enough books for all students? Are the most current editions in use?

_____

_____

_____

_____

_____

7. What is the accountability structure for teachers in terms of improving student outcomes?

_____

_____

_____

_____

_____

8. How are state and federal accountability standards monitored?

_____

_____

_____

_____

_____

9. What career-technical courses or pathways does the district offer? Have there been attempts to integrate technical and academic coursework?

_____

_____

_____

_____

_____

Please write down the textbook used for each subject listed in the table for each high school. If the same book is used at all high schools, please indicate so.

Textbooks

	High School 1	High School 2	High School 3	High School 4
English ninth				
English tenth				
English eleventh				
English twelfth				
Algebra I				
Geometry				
Algebra II				
World history				
U.S. history				
Civics				
Economics				
Biology				
Chemistry				
Physics				
Other				

HUMAN RESOURCE SURVEY

Please provide answers to the following questions related to information on the teacher capacity to implement college and career readiness. A teacher who holds more than one credential should be put into the one that you feel fits best. Do not count a teacher twice.

Math Analysis

1. How many high school math teachers are needed for all students to take the full college-preparatory sequence in math? _____
2. How many teachers in the district are currently qualified to teach algebra, geometry, algebra II, and beyond? _____
3. Subtract 2 from 1 for total need _____
4. Factor out the anticipated retirement of this cohort to determine the numbers of new teachers needed over time _____
5. Estimate the gap _____

Science Analysis

1. How many high school science teachers are needed for all students to take a college-preparatory sequence in science? _____
2. How many teachers in the district are currently qualified to teach biology, chemistry, physics, and beyond? _____
3. Subtract 2 from 1 for total need _____
4. Factor out the anticipated retirement of this cohort to determine the numbers of new teachers needed over time _____
5. Estimate the gap _____

World Language Analysis

1. How many high school language teachers are needed for all students to have at least two years of a common world language? _____
2. How many teachers in the district are currently qualified to teach a world language? _____
3. Subtract 2 from 1 for total need _____
4. Factor out the anticipated retirement of this cohort to determine the number of new teachers needed over time _____
5. Estimate the gap _____

FACILITIES SURVEY

Please provide information on the state of the science laboratories in the district to determine if sufficient numbers of stations exist to offer lab sciences to all students. In order to be considered a lab facility, a space must be able to accommodate biology, chemistry, or physics work. A station is usually a table or island with a sink, which can accommodate at least four students.

Districtwide	School 1	School 2	School 3	School 4
Number of students: _____	Number of students: _____	Number of students: _____	Number of students: _____	Number of students: _____
Number of lab facilities: _____	Number of lab facilities: _____	Number of lab facilities: _____	Number of lab facilities: _____	Number of lab facilities: _____

PROFESSIONAL DEVELOPMENT

Please answer the following questions about district- and site-driven in-service training activities.

1. What is the vision of professional development for the district? Do the district and schools have a written professional development plan?

_____

_____

_____

_____

_____

2. Provide a list of professional development activities from last year.

_____

_____

_____

_____

_____

3. What are some examples of sustained professional development?

_____

_____

_____

_____

_____

4. How much time is devoted to teacher collaboration? What is the structure of this time? Districtwide? Site based?

_____

_____

_____

_____

_____

5. What accommodations are provided for external professional development in terms of time and money?

_____

_____

_____

_____

6. What standards-based training has been provided for teachers? Describe when and what the training was.

_____

_____

_____

_____

_____

7. What training has been provided for teachers of English learners? Describe when and what the training was.

_____

_____

_____

_____

_____

8. What training has been provided for differentiated instruction? Describe when and what the training was.

_____

_____

_____

_____

_____

9. What subject-matter training has been provided? Describe when and what the training was.

_____

_____

_____

_____

_____

10. How are career-technical teachers supported? What type of professional development is available to these teachers? How do career-technical teachers and regular education teachers collaborate?

_____

_____

_____

_____

_____

SAFETY NET AND SUPPORT INTERVENTIONS SURVEY

Please answer the questions about the services you are providing to struggling students.

1. What safety nets and intervention programs are currently offered to high school students? How many students are serviced by these programs? How long are students involved in these programs? How are they identified? Please fill in the following table.

Program	Number of Students	Length	Short Description of How Students Are Identified
Advancement Via Individual Determination (AVID) and AVID-like programs			
Gaining Early Awareness and Readiness for Under-graduate Programs (GearUp) and Math, Engineering, Science Achievement (MESA) type of programs			
Shadow classes and extended blocks			
College outreach			
Extra classes for struggling students			
Saturday academies			
After-school programs			
Mentoring			
Tutoring			
Other interventions			

2. Is there a Summer Bridge program for incoming freshman who need a jump-start on high school? How many students take part in this program? How is their progress monitored afterward?

_____

_____

_____

3. What is the protocol for summer school enrollment? How is placement determined for classes? Is summer school mandatory for students? Which students?

_____

_____

_____

4. Are there drop-in tutoring opportunities for students? What is the structure? Is it mandatory? Is there study hall time? What is the structure?

_____

_____

_____

5. What counseling services are available for struggling students?

_____

_____

_____

6. Are there just-in-time interventions in place to catch students who start to slip in their academic coursework? What role do benchmark assessments play in providing curricular interventions?

_____

_____

_____

7. Do schools have advisory periods? If so, what is the schedule for the advisory period? What is the structure for the advisory period? Can students choose any teacher or advisor to go to? Is the advisory period mandatory for all students? If not, how do students qualify for the advisory?

_____

_____

_____

SPECIAL EDUCATION, ALTERNATIVE EDUCATION, AND ENGLISH LEARNER SURVEY

Please answer the following questions about access to college and career preparation for special education students, alternative education students, and English language learners.

1. List the programs and services provided for special education and alternative education students and English learners.

   _____

   _____

   _____

2. If a differentiated diploma is given to any of these populations, how does it differ from a regular diploma?

   _____

   _____

   _____

3. What accommodations are currently in place to allow special populations access to a regular high school diploma?

   _____

   _____

   _____

4. What accommodations are currently in place to allow special populations access to college-preparatory coursework?

   _____

   _____

   _____

CAREER TECHNICAL EDUCATION (CTE) SURVEY

Please fill in the table with information on the range of career pathways offered by the high schools. Place an *X* in the appropriate boxes.

CTE Pathway	High School 1	High School 2	High School 3	High School 4
Agricultural and natural sciences				
Arts, media, and entertainment				
Building trades and construction				
Education, child development, and family services				
Energy and utilities				
Engineering and design				
Fashion and interior design				
Finance and business				
Health science and medical technology				
Hospitality, tourism, and recreation				
Information technology				
Manufacturing and product development				
Marketing, sales, and service				
Public services				
Transportation				

INDEX

Public engagement strategy: at San Jose Unified School District, 23–24; work of district departments regarding, 89